Trojan War

A Guide of Survival During the Trojan War

(Literature and Legends From the Bronze Age to the Present)

Marion McCauley

Published By **Bella Frost**

Marion McCauley

All Rights Reserved

Trojan War: A Guide of Survival During the Trojan War (Literature and Legends From the Bronze Age to the Present)

ISBN 978-1-77485-485-3

No part of this guidebook shall be reproduced in any form without permission in writing from the publisher except in the case of brief quotations embodied in critical articles or reviews.

Legal & Disclaimer

The information contained in this ebook is not designed to replace or take the place of any form of medicine or professional medical advice. The information in this ebook has been provided for educational & entertainment purposes only.

The information contained in this book has been compiled from sources deemed reliable, and it is accurate to the best of the Author's knowledge; however, the Author cannot guarantee its accuracy and validity and cannot be held liable for any errors or omissions. Changes are periodically made to this book. You must consult your doctor or get professional medical advice before using any of the suggested remedies, techniques, or information in this book.

Upon using the information contained in this book, you agree to hold harmless the Author from and against any damages, costs, and expenses, including any legal fees potentially resulting from the application of any of the information provided by this guide. This disclaimer applies to any damages or injury caused by the use and application, whether directly or indirectly, of any advice or information presented, whether for breach of contract, tort, negligence, personal injury, criminal intent, or under any other cause of action.

You agree to accept all risks of using the information presented inside this book. You need to consult a professional medical practitioner in order to ensure you are both able and healthy enough to participate in this program.

TABLE OF CONTENTS

INTRODUCTION 1

CHAPTER 1: A SHORT INTRODUCTION TO ANCIENT GREECE, GREEKS AND THEIR FAITH 3

CHAPTER 2: THE ORIGINS 11

CHAPTER 3: GODS, GODDESSES AND SPIRITS 21

CHAPTER 4: MONSTERS, HYBRIDS & GIANTS................... 32

CHAPTER 5: SHORT TALES OF HEROES............................. 34

CHAPTER 6: PROMETHEUS 59

CHAPTER 7: PANDORA'S BOX 61

CHAPTER 8: OEDIPUS AND THE SELF-FULFILLING PROPHECY 66

CHAPTER 9: THE BATTLES 73

CHAPTER 10: THE ODYSSEY 85

CHAPTER 11: THE SEEDS OF STRIFE.................................. 93

CHAPTER 12: HEADING TO WAR 107

CHAPTER 13: LOGISTICS... 155

CHAPTER 14: MYTH, LEGEND, OR FOLKTALE?................ 160

CHAPTER 15: THEMES.. 168

CHAPTER 16: HOW WOULD YOU IMAGINE THAT THE ANCIENT GREEKS HAVE WORSHIPED THESE GODS? 175

Introduction

Humans have long been seeking understand their place within the universe. We've always wanted to understand our origins and the origins of the universe that surrounds us as well as the universe's origins and why different things work how they do. We are interested in knowing who is the one who runs the universe, who decides the things that happen and how we are placed into the overall picture. These "explanations" have for an extended period of time been handed down through generations in various forms. While the societies of the time regarded the stories as true but everyone else considers it to be a myth and consider them myths. The interesting thing is that these tales are refined that they can have a lot of meaning even in a contemporary view.

Of all the mythologies around the world, Greek mythology is by all means among the most fascinating and captivating. The history of ancient Greece as well as Greek mythology are fascinating and if you'd like to learn more about the subject then this book is the one ideal for you. The book offers a comprehensive look into the nature of Greek mythology is, and what it encompasses, as well as the major Gods, Goddesses, heroes, titans , and monsters that are the governing force.

Chapter 1: A Short Introduction to Ancient Greece, Greeks And Their Faith

Before moving onto Greek mythology, it's crucial to shed some light on the past of Greece since that's the reason why it gave the mythology its birth.

Ancient Greece

Greece in the way we see it today, wasn't always this way when we read the books on history. The present-day Greece is only a tiny part of what is now Ancient Greece which is frequently called mainland Greece.

The truth is, Ancient Greece was not just a part of mainland Greece It was also extended across the world, comprising Spain, Italy (including Sicily), France, Egypt, Turkey, Romania, Bulgaria, Syria, Libya and

Ukraine. For more than 40,000 years people lived in Ancient Greece following a lifestyle of harvesting, hunting, or farming.

But, the first major civilization that has existed in Greece is known as Minoans. The Minoans lived between 2200BC and 1450 BC under their famous ruler "Minos." After the Minoans, another important civilization emerged from mainland Greece and was named Mycenaean.

The Mycenaean period ended around 1100 BC at the time that Greece went into an Dark Age that lasted for 300 years. There isn't a written document or artwork that describes what transpired during this Dark Age.

The archaic period began around 800BC. period, which continued until 480BC. In this period, many cities in Greece were controlled by king-like figures.

Around the year 480BC Greece was able to enter a golden period that lasted for around 200 years.

The period that ended Greek history is known as the Hellenistic period. It was the time when Romans were in control of Greece and ran from 323BC until 30 BC. The Romans revered Greek culture. Greek tradition and were able to adopt a lot aspects of Greek beliefs. The Romans also copied numerous other aspects from Greek culture , including clothing, structures, and even their religious beliefs.

Through the course of Greek time there was never any country that could be called "Ancient Greece"; instead there were city-states of a smaller size like Athens, Sparta, Olympia and Troy. The city-states had the laws of their respective governments and armies. The citizens of these cities-states are called Greeks. But, Greeks considered their loyalty to their city-state first, and Greece as a second.

Thus, those who lived in Athens identified themselves as Athenians first, and Greek second. Since the loyalty of citizens was based on their city-states first and foremost, there was a lot of conflict between different states, leading states to wage war against their own. But, at times, states would unite in battle against a bigger adversary like that of the Persian Empire.

In spite of all conflicts, Greeks had a set of common religious beliefs which nearly all were a part of. This is known as Greek Mythology.

Understanding Greek Mythology

Greek Mythology is the set of stories and myths that the people from Ancient Greece considered to be myths regarding their gods, heroes and their origins, as well as the nature of the world they lived in, and the significance of their rituals.

While Greek Mythology dates back to 2000 BC, it began to grow in the 700s with the appearance of three epic poetry: Iliad and Odyssey by Homer and Theogony by Hesiod.

These poems contain a selection of myths Ancient Greeks believed and lived by. The most popular myths include the following.

Mount Olympus - The Home of Gods

Greeks believe they believed that Mount Olympus was the home of Gods that were created after the battle known as Titanomachy that was fought by the Titans who were a group of Greek Gods prior to the time that Olympians became the rulers.

The belief was that Gods resided in a palace that was high up over the clouds on Mount Olympus. But, Gods were not limited to a certain area of Mount Olympus; they could wander around in the open.

Worshipping Beliefs

Greeks believed that Gods guard their people from the comfort of their homes and sometimes intervene in their daily life below. If Gods weren't happy with mortals, they could summon an enraged storm in order to wipe out the entire city, or to ensure that their beloved mortals win in the war. This is the reason Ancient Greeks build temples to worship Gods and offered sacrifices to animals to keep them content.

Each city that were located within Greece had a goddess as a patron or God who protected the inhabitants from danger. If the need arose, people would visit the temples to pray to the Gods. This helped keep their patron God content to prevent massive chaos in the streets.

Life After Death

Greeks were also believers in existence of a life after death. It was believed by them that dead passed to an underground kingdom referred to by the name of "The underworld." The belief was that the souls of the deceased had to traverse the River Styx to reach the Underworld.

To traverse the River Styx, the soul of the deceased was required to pay a furious ferryman dubbed Charon. This is why Greeks typically put a penny in the mouth of the deceased to allow his soul to traverse the river to reach the Underworld.

When a soul reaches the Underworld The soul's destiny to live forever is determined in three years by three judges. If the soul was very good throughout its the world, it could be content within the Elysian Fields. If it was good and had a good life, it could spend the all of its time in the place known as Asphodel Meadows. But, if the person was a bad person all through his life and his soul was rotting, then it will be sucked into the pit of hell known as Tartarus.

After having a basic understanding of an overview of Greeks and the mythological stories they tell we can take this discussion to a greater extent.

Like in the same way that the Christian Bible starts from the beginning (Genesis) i.e. the time when God made the heavens as well as the earth , then created man on the sixth day, it is believed that the Greeks have their own version which explains how the universe was created. This is what we'll learn in the next section.

Chapter 2: The Origins

To fully comprehend Greek mythology, you need to know the source of the universe which Ancient Greeks believed. I'll shed some light on this during this article.

God's First Generation First Generation of Gods

At first there was nothing other than Chaos (something that was dark and shapeless). What Chaos was and the form it took isn't clear but we do know that it was the source of the essential elemental gods.

From Chaos Five gods came in existence. Gaia (mother Earth), Nyx also known as Night (darkness over the earth), Tartarus (underworld), Erebus (darkness covering underworld) as well as Eros (Love). But, there isn't a specific reason in Greek mythology as to the way these gods were created from Chaos.

Gaia was the mother of Uranus (the Sky) which was a blanket that covered Gaia from all angles. At the same time, Erebus and Night came together, and gave birth to Hemera (Day), Doom, Phos (Light) and Misery, Deceit Death, and a jolly group of quintuplets. Then, Discord was the birthplace of Murder, Crime, Battle, and Slaughter.

Birth of Monsters and Giants

Gaia (female) Gaia (female) and Uranus (male) got married and had their three first children, which were later revealed to be Hekatoncheires (Monsters). They each had strong hands of 100 and 50 heads that were unexpected for their families. They tried to fix their mistakes and had a second sex, however the results were too different since they had three Cyclopes (Giants).

The Cyclopes were superior to the previous experiments however they were not completely
perfect. Cyclopes were massive one-eyed giants, who were extremely

strong and could be as massive as mountains. The three Cyclopes comprised Brontes, Arges and Steropes.

Birth Of The Titans (Second Generation Of Gods)

When Gaia along with Uranus were the parents of their first 6 children who were later revealed to be giants and monsters Then they reverted their mistakes and had a second batch of 12 children who were named Oceanus (God of the Sea), Hyperion (God of the Sun), Thetis, Rhea, Iapetus, Mnemosyne (Goddess of Memory), Themis, Theia, Phoebe, Coeus, Crius, Cronos (God of Time). The children, along with other siblings and brothers were referred to as the Titans which turned out to be healthy and their second generations of Gods and Goddesses.

Gaia's Revenge

Uranus was a terrible wife and father. He wasn't enthralled by the thought of having children and, when each became born, Uranus forced the babies back to Gaia alive, which made her become a maniac. She decided to get revenge on Uranus and demanded her children assist her. Her son Cronos whom she considered to be the smartest of his Titan sisters and brothers, was willing to assist his mother.

Gaia produced a sickle of flint which was massive in size, and gave it to Cronos with specific instructions. When Uranus was about to mat with Gaia in ignorance of the plot to retaliate against Gaia, he was snatched by Cronos. Cronos who was in Gaia's womb reached for the sickle, and cut off the Genitals of his father. He then toss them into the ocean.

When Uranus' blood spilled, it created other giants and monsters. The genitals of Uranus that fell into the ocean the water froze and out of the foam goddess Aphrodite became a reality. The goddess floated on the sea for a while before she was able to emerge on the shore of Cyprus This is the reason why she is known as Cyprian Aphrodite.

Uranus' fate Uranus following that time isn't evident, whether he perished or escaped from the earth, we do not know for sure. But, upon his departure Uranus said to ensure that Titans and Cronos were to be punished. Following Uranus lost, Cronos was declared the supreme ruler as well as leader over the Titans. He was married to the sister of his Rhea.

The birth of the Olympians (Third Generation of Gods)

When Cronos was the ruler, Cronos had numerous offspring along from his marriage to Rhea. He ate the entire family when they were born in order in order to avoid the prophecy that was proclaimed by his parents and father. The prophecy said "he will be destroyed by his own children."

Rhea was furious at the way Cronos was treating her child. She hid her face at the time of the birth of her sixth child , 'Zeus' and put him on Crete. Crete to be taken care of by Nymphs. Nymphs were spirits regarded as beautiful women who inhabited forests, rivers and different locations.

To hide what she did to conceal what she did, she covered a stone with clothes and handed it over to Cronos and then inhaled it, assuming that it was his child.

Zeus was born on Crete free from the grip by his dad. Nymphs fed him, and minor Gods hit their spears every time Zeus was crying, so that Cronos would not be able to hear his cry. Zeus was a beautiful man, and Rhea got Cronos to believe in Zeus. He was then allowed to go again in Mount Olympus to become the cup bearer of Cronos.

Zeus was not a fan of his father since Zeus had no reason to act in that manner. So, he went to his mother

Gaia and made special drinks for Cronos which caused him to throw his children that he taken. When Cronos began vomiting, the very first thing to come out was the stone was swallowed, believing that it was his sixth.

Then, he let go of the other five children who have grown in his stomach and ascended as gods. These gods, together with Zeus and other Gods were referred to as the Olympians. The names of these gods were: Hera (Goddess of marriage), Hades (God of underworld), Demeter (Goddess of harvest and crops), Poseidon (God of Sea) as well as Hestia (Goddess of the hearth).

The Rise of Zeus and the Olympians

When the Olympians were released from Cronos and offered their thanks to the god of their brothers Zeus and acknowledged Cronos as their ruler, however, Cronos was not yet defeated. Cronos fought to keep his supremacy. His Titan siblings and brothers aided them, with the exception of Prometheus, Oceanus and Epimetheus. Atlas was the first chief of the Titans in the fight to take down one of the lesser Gods.

Zeus was clever similar to his grandfather. He rescued Cyclopes as well as Hekatoncheires of Tartarus who were held there as punishments from Cronos after Zeus defeated Uranus. Prometheus was also a part of Zeus which strengthened him since Zeus gained new allies along with Cyclopes Hekatoncheires as well as Prometheus.

Zeus defeated Cronos and Titans together with Zeus' new friends. Zeus used lightning bolts as weapons supplied by Cyclopes. The Hekatoncheires created an ambush for Titans and Zeus was able to retreat from the fight to take to lead the Titans to the trap that was set by Hekatoncheires. While the Titans were snatched, Hekatoncheires threw hundreds of boulders over them in the force of the mountains were falling upon them. They ran off, leaving Zeus the victor.

Following winning the battle of Zeus He exiled the Titans to Tartarus but not their leader Atlas who was punished to ensnare the entire whole world upon his back. The imprisonment of her children caused Gaea unhappy, so Gaea gave birth to her final child Typhoeous that was terrifying that the majority of Gods left. But, Zeus faced the monster and defeated it with assistance with lightning bolts. Zeus was burial in Sicily beneath Mount Etna.

Then Zeus's rule was questioned from Giants (born by Uranus' testicles removed through Cronos) who tried to conquer Mount Olympus by piling mountain upon mountain , but with the aid of Heracles and Heracles, the Giants were killed as well. Following the conflict, Zeus married Metis.

Like his father, Zeus also received a prophecy from his wife that she would have a child that will be the

King of the Gods. To dispel the prophecy Zeus swallowed his wife. However, the baby was born nonetheless. The name of the child was Athena and she emerged through Zeus's head. Zeus. However, Zeus wasn't at risk due to her birth since her birth didn't include an important part of the prophecy that included: Metis will bear a child.

But, Athena had the cunning ability that her mom had. Later, she would be the goddess of craft practical reason, war and handicraft and was unable to be violated by other goddesses.

If you now have an understanding of the history of Greek gods and goddesses and an understanding of mythology, let's move this discussion to the next level by understanding the traits of gods, goddesses and titans, giants , and the mythical beasts.

Chapter 3: Gods, Goddesses and Spirits

To fully comprehend Greek mythology, you need to be aware of the different kinds of Gods and Goddesses. The following are three kinds of Gods and Goddesses that Ancient Greeks believed in. Understanding these will strengthen your understanding of Greek Mythology.

Protogenoi (Primordial Gods)

The first kind of Gods in Greek Mythology is called Protogenoi. The name comes by two Greek words "Protos" refers to "First" while "Genos" is a reference to birth. The Gods of the Old Testament were the very first born creatures that were fully formed during the creation process and created the very material of the universe. The Gods of the elemental realm are: Gaia (Earth), Ananke (Necessity), Uranus (Sky) Hemera (Day) Tethys (Nursing), Nyx (Night), Ourea (Mountains), Pontus (Sea), Oceanus (Water) and numerous others.

While these Gods were pure elemental beings but they could also be depicted in human-like forms. For instance, in certain old paintings, Gaia might appear as an anthropomorphic woman, with her upper part rising out of the earth but inseparable from her basic appearance.

Theoi Gods

The second kind of Gods is known as Theoi Gods whose responsibility was to confer civilized arts on humanity and to control the nature forces. They can further be classified into eight categories , which include: Titan Gods, Olympian Gods, Sky Gods, Underworld Gods, Sea Gods,

Agricultural Earth Gods, City Gods and Pastoral Earth Gods. In all, Titans and Olympians were the most well-known and that's why I'll go over a few Titan Gods.

Titan Gods

Titan Gods were the second generation of Gods who rule the universe following the demise by Uranus (A Primordial God of the Sky). While there were several Titans but the most famous ones are the group of 12 daughters and sons of Uranus and the four children of Iapetus (God of Mortality); Atlas, Epimetheus, Prometheus and Menoetius. I'll look at a few of the most prominent Titans here.

Cronos

Cronos was the original God in Time and also the King of the Titans. He was king after defeating the father of his time, Uranus.

Rhea

Rhea was the wife and sister of Cronos and was regarded as the queen of heaven during the golden age of the time during the time that Cronos was King. She was the goddess of fertility, motherhood and the generation.

Oceanus

Oceanus was a god of the primordial era of the fresh waters. The oceanus god was also God of fresh water. He was the God who also had the power to regulate heavens which rose and set out from his water.

Iapetus

Iapetus is the name given to him by Uranus as well as Gaea and was the father of Atlas, Epimetheus, Prometheus and Menoetius. He was often referred to by the name of God of Craftsmanship and was often referred to as the God of Mortality.

Atlas

Atlas is the name given to him by Iapetus and was the God of navigation and astronomy. Atlas was the leader of the Titans who were fighting Titanomachy (war in which Titans as well as Olympians). But, he was on the losing side and was given the punishment of carrying all the weight of earth upon his shoulders.

Prometheus

Prometheus was the twin brother of Atlas and is referred by God. God who created the universe. In the fight of Titanomachy Prometheus was a supporter of Zeus and ended up on the winning side. But, he was in battle with Zeus as he attempted to help the people of the world. Prometheus's story is significant in Greek mythology. I'll be discussing the individual stories in a different chapter as well.

Epimetheus

Epimetheus was a second Titan and was the son of Prometheus who was a part of Zeus on Titanomachy. He was appointed by Zeus to give gifts to the earthly creatures. He was in love with Pandora which was the reason that mankind received hope as a present.

Olympian Gods

The Olympians were the third generation of Gods who ruled after having defeated the rule of Cronos in the battle of Titanomachy. While there were numerous Olympian Gods, there were twelve whom are called the great Gods.

The most powerful Olympian Gods are:

Zeus

Poseidon (God of the Sea Earthquakes, Floods, and Poseidon)

Apollo (God of Oracles, Prophecy and Prophecy) Plague, Disease and healing)

Aphrodite (Goddess of Beauty, Love, Pleasure and Procreation)

Demeter (Goddess of the Agriculture)

Hephaestus (God from fire)

Ares (God of the War, Courage and the Civil Order)

Hermes (God for Hospitality Hermes (God of Hospitality and Travel)

Artemis (Goddess from Wilderness hunting, Hunting as well as Wild Animals)

Hera (Goddess of the Marriage)

Athena (Goddess in Counsel as well as Wisdom)

Dionysus (God of Wine, Vegetation, and Celebration)

Of these 12, Zeus is probably the most well-known, therefore I'm going to talk about Zeus in detail.

Zeus

Zeus was the god of Cronos and is known as God of Sky the King, Law as well as Order, Destiny and

Fate. Zeus was crowned the King of Olympian Gods after Zeus defeated his father, and liberated his sisters and brothers from Cronos. Zeus was the youngest of children from Cronos as well as Rhea (Titans queen and King, respectively).

Spirits (Daimones)

The third kind of Gods in Greek Mythology is called Spirits (Daimones). They were the souls of righteous men, who were immortal in the nature. Spirits are further divided into three categories which include:

Nature Spirits

The first kind of spirits was referred to as spirits of nature. The spirits, along with Nymphs were nourished by four main elements: dryads of the forest, fresh water naiads love satyrs, marine tritons, etc.

Constellation Spirits

The second kind of immortal spirits were the spirits of constellations who made their way through the heavens (night skies). Each constellation was affected by at least one spirit. It also encompasses the 12 Zodiac signs. For instance, Sagittarius was influenced by the spirit of the Centaur Kheiron.

The Body and Mind Impact Spirits

The third and the most important kind of spirits is called the mind and body that affect spirits. They controlled abstract ideas in our minds as well as the physical bodily conditions of the human bodies. These spirits' names were capitalized nouns. For instance"love" was referred to as "Eros" and is an Greek word meaning love. The most important spirits from Greek Mythology are listed below as well as their domains.

Eros (Goddess of Love)

Dike (Goddess in Justice and Fair Judgment and justice)

Eris (Goddess to Discord as well as Rivalry)

Geras (Goddess in Old Age)

Hebe (Goddess of Youth)

Hygeia (Goddess of Health)

Hypnos (God of Sleep)

Lyssa (Goddess with fury and anger in animals)

Mnemosyne (Goddess of Memory)

Nemesis (Goddess Of Indignation)

Nike (Goddess of Victory)

Peitho (Goddess of Persuasion)

Phobos (God of Fear)

Ploutus (God of Wealth)

Poine (Goddess of Retaliation)

Pictures (God of Sexual Desire)

Soteria (Goddess of Safety)

Thanatos (God for non-violent Death)

Greek mythology is not complete without the inclusion of monsters, giants, and hybrids which play a significant part in the story. The next chapter will discuss them.

Chapter 4: Monsters, Hybrids & Giants

The story of Greek Mythology, there are other gods, goddesses, and spirits. They were referred to as giants, monsters, and hybrids which were semi-divine in nature , and often linked in a close way to Gods. Below are a few of the creatures which have significance within Greek Mythology.

Typhoons

Typhoeous was a massive monster, known as a winged beast that had a head that touched the stars. Typhoeous was the child of Gaea who was born to get revenge on Zeus who had slain the sons of her (Titans) from heaven and punished the tyrants through sending them back to Tartarus. Then, Typhoeous was killed by Zeus through lightning bolts.

Hekatoncheires

Hekatoncheires were the three first children from Gaea as well as Uranus. They were giants with fifty heads, and 100 fingers. They were released through Zeus from Tartarus because they were confined there during the time of Titans who ruled the world. As a recompense they attacked Titans in Titanomachy and caused Titans to lose their battle.

Sphinx

Sphinx was female hybrid with a head and breasts were similar to women, and the remainder of her body resembled the lion's wings. Sphinx was sent into Thebes in the hands of Gods to be punished for an offence. She took her own life after she came across Oedipus (detail that is later mentioned in the book).

Cyclopes

Cyclopes were three one eyed immortal giants that were the children of Gaea and Uranus. Uranus was able to force them back into Gaea when the three were being born. Then, Titans took them out of Gaea and sent them to Tartarus. Through Titanomachy, Zeus freed them from Tartarus and they returned the favor by making lightning bolts to Zeus to use against Titans that brought him victory.

After you have figured out who the most prominent characters from Greek mythology I'll share with you some famous tales that tell of Gods as well as heroes.

Chapter 5: Short Tales of Heroes

Greek Mythology is full of heroes that are either daughters or sons of Gods themselves , and are sometimes called gods. A lot of these heroes gained their respect due to their an adventurous life that turned them into legendary after their deaths. There are a myriad of heroes from Greek Mythology, but I will discuss the most well-known heroes and their stories within this volume.

The most famous heroes from Greek mythology are Achilles, Hercules and Odysseus. Odysseus The story of Odysseus is discussed in the next chapter. This is why I'll focus on the two other protagonists in this section.

Achilles

Achilles was the child of Peleus and Thetis. Thetis was a sea nymph while Peleus was the ruler of Myrmidons. At the time of the birth of Achilles, a prophecy appeared that he would be either destined to live an enlightened and prosperous life without any adventures it or die young during the war and become an icon. To avoid this His mother took him to the River Styx when he was just a baby and immersed into it in order to make him immortal.

She didn't realize the fact that her heel she was holding was not in contact with water, so it was the only part of Achilles' body that was harmed and eventually became the cause for his demise when the arrow he was shooting hit him with an arrow with poisonous poison right in the heel.

Achilles played an important part in his role during the Trojan War where he led 2500 Myrmidons and killed the most skilled soldier from Troy Hector, which was the prince from Troy. In addition, prior to reaching Troy He stopped in Tenedos to kill their King, who was a demigod as his father was God Apollo.

He was also one of the factors behind how the Greeks discovered the path to Troy by helping Telephus (King of Mysia) after he gave him a wound which could only be treated by his assistance. Telephus was given the metal from his spear. In an act of retribution Telephus also told Telephus how to get to Troy.

Jason

Jason is an Greek hero who is most famously well-known as the Argonauts' leader. an adventurers' group in the search of the Golden Fleece. While they were successful in their endeavor, Jason never fulfilled his goal of becoming the King of Iolcus which was his rightful birthright.

He was always his father Aeson the king of Iolcus However, there are some different opinions on the nature of his mother's identity. It is known that, when he was an infant His grandfather Pelias killed all of the children of Aeson, and then overthrew his father. The only one he killed was Jason. His mother was able to save Jason from the wailing of Jason by having the midwives huddle around him and it appears the child was stillborn. He was later taken to Chiron who was a centaur to learn. Pelias was still frightened of being usurped , she consulted an oracle who predicted his being snubbed by a man wearing only one sandal.

A few years later, Jason is back to Iolcus as a bid to claim his title as the heir to the crown. The king arrived to Iolcus in the course of a game competition Pelias held in honour of Poseidon and was declared "the man who wore only just one shoe." Jason lost his sandal as he tried to help an elderly lady to cross the stream (the goddess Hera disguised). Jason bravely approached Pelias and demanded to be removed in the knowledge that the king's rightful position. Pelias acknowledged his request but gave him a task to locate his Golden Fleece to cede the throne.

The Argonauts

Jason set up a team comprised of around fifty heroes, referred to as the Argonauts named after the name Jason's boat, Argo. Some notable names of the crew of the ship include: Heracles, Theseus, Laertes - father of Odysseus, Autolycus - A master thief, and Son of Hermes, Peleus - father of Achilles, Orpheus - the legendary hero musician, and the Castor twins - Brothers to Helen and Helen of Troy.

The Golden Fleece was in the Conchils region, which was distant. In order to get there the Argonauts needed to travel through:

*The Isle of Lemnos - which was home to a tribe of women referred to as Minyae. Jason was the father of twins who were born to the queen of their race, Hypsipyle.

*The Land Of The Doliones - The Dolione King Cyzicus was kind to them. A accident between the Argonauts and Doliones led to the deaths of Cyzicus and his queen.

* The Court of Phineus Of Salmydessus in Thrace in exchange to help chase these flying creatures Harpies, Phineus told them the exact location of Colchis.

* The Symplegades also called The closing rock, are two massive rock cliffs which joined and crushed anything that went between them. Phineus also gave them advice on how to cross the Symplegades with the help of a dove.

The Argonauts finally made it to Colchis in order to take possession of Colchis to claim the Golden Fleece, which is held by the King Aeetes from Colchis. Aeetes accepted to allow Jason take the fleece provided he can complete three seemingly impossible tasks:

* Mow a field using an ox with a flame-breathing fire

* Sow dragon's teeth into the field, and fight the army that springs up from it.

• Overcome the sleepless dragon who was guarding the Golden Fleece

Jason completed his work with the assistance of Medea who was Medea, King Aeetes his daughter who was in love with Jason. Medea was a brilliant woman and a powerful sorcerer and had only aided Jason to repay his love for him that was never ending. After recovering the fleece the Argo left Colchis with Medea aboard.

After a long trip filled with adventures along the route, the Argonauts returned to Iolcus. Medea was able to help Jason to kill Pelias by cutting him into pieces (by the daughters of his) into tiny pieces and the boiled his body. The shocking murder caused the inhabitants of Iolcus flee the scene. The couple relocated to Corinth where they stayed for ten years. They also were blessed with two children.

Death and later life

At Corinth, Jason tried to increase his influence in the political arena by getting married to Creusa his daughter and King. Believing he had been betrayed, Medea killed the princess with the help of witchcraft. The king also lost his life the attempt to rescue his princess. She also killed two sons she had to Jason before fleeing to Athens.

Jason spent his final days in Corinth in solitude, broken by the tragedy. There are rumors that Medea killed Jason in the course of her bloody battle.

Perseus

Perseus is among the most revered heroes of Greek Mythology. He is best known for the one who killed the Gorgon Medusa and a terrifying monster, and for the hero who saved the Ethiopian princess Andromeda from the sea monster Cetus.

Perseus was the god of Zeus and the mortal, Danae, the daughter of Acrisius the the king of Argos. An interview with an Oracle at Delphi will reveal that Danae is going to bear one son that will ultimately take the King's life. Incredulous, Acrisius locks Danae in an open bronze chamber up to heaven. Zeus notices

Danae trapped in the room and is attracted to her. Zeus visits Danae with an oath of gold and then impregnates her. Acrisius in furious is able to lock Danae along with Perseus inside a chest, and throws them into the ocean. Luckily, they float towards the island Serifos and are received by a fisherman named Dictys. Dictys took care of the tiny Perseus as his own and looks after his mother.

The King of the island, Polydectes loves with Danae however Perseus hinders his attempts to impress his mother, as Perseus doesn't believe in his son. Convinced that there is no way to be able to win the heart of Danae by keeping Perseus in his life, Polydectes comes up with an idea.

Medusa

Polydectes invites his pals (Perseus not excluded) at his birthday celebration and asks them to each give him a horse for gifts. Perseus could not pay for a horse, and he promises to present the king with something to replace it. Polydectes formally requests him to give his head the Gorgon in the hope of being killed.The Gorgons are three beasts with hairs of snakes, and eyes that could turn people to stone. Only one of the three, Medusa, was a mortal.

Proud and adventurous, Perseus sets out to complete the task by enlisting the assistance of gods Athena, Zeus, and Hermes. He discovers The Graeae, three nasty females with teeth and an eye. After some naughty arguments and a few tries, they reveal the place of the Hesperides three nymphs who are charged with the protection of gods' most precious objects. They also give him

* Zeus' adamantine sword

* Hades"helmet of darkness" (invisibility cloak)

* Hermes"winged sandals" to fly

The polished shield of Athena

* Kibisis is a knapsack that will stop Medusa's head safe from bleeding poisonous blood

Fully equipped with all the necessary equipment, he embarks on his quest and finds the Gorgons cave. He crawls through the cave by making use of the mirror on his polished shield. He beheads the asleep Medusa by using his sword. He escapes the two others, Stheno and Euryale, by hiding in Hades his invisibility helmet and flying using Hermes and his sandals. He then keeps his head inside Kibisis and then heads back to home. When he returns to home, he is involved in an dispute with Atlas (remember the punishment imposed on him by Zeus to carry the entire globe on his back) He refuses to give him protection. Perseus takes him down by turning his body into stone with Medusa's head. He also saves Princess Andromeda in the process of returning. We'll briefly discuss the story in the future.

After he returns home, he discovers his mother in a temple far from the beautiful Polydectes. He killed Polydectes and his comrades using the gorgon's skull, making Dictys the island's king and then returned all the presents to Hesperides. In regard to Medusa's head He presents his impressive trophy as a sign of gratitude to Athena.

Andromeda

Andromeda was the son of King Cepheus and Queen Cassiopeia of Ethiopia. They had drawn the wrath of Poseidon because they boasted that their daughter was prettier than sea Nymphs. This insult irritates Poseidon and he sent Cetus the sea serpent to ruin the earth. A Oracle tells us that the only method Cetus could be soothed is to make a sacrifice of Andromeda for him. So she was pinned by chains to a rock on the beach in a state of waiting for her death by the Sea monster Poseidon. That was the state she was discovered by Perseus while he was on his way home from his trip to the Gorgons cave. Perseus defeated the beast following a brutal battles with the aid of Medusa's head as well as Pegasus. He weds Andromeda and turns her angry former lover, Phineus, to stone and then returns back to his home on Serifos. Island in Serifos.

The Second Life, Death and the Afterlife

After the installation of Dictys as the King of Serifos, Perseus and his family decided to return home to Argos. They kept their move secret from his father, King Acrisius. One day, Perseus was killed by the King in an discus throw incident during an athletic competition. The prophecy had been fulfilled!

Not feeling worthy of the throne after causing the loss of his grandpa, he sold Argos' Kingdom Argos for Megapenthes to acquire Megapenthes" kingdom of Tiryns.

Perseus along with his spouse Andromeda are happily settled in

Tiryns. In Tiryns, following an extended and prosperous time in power, Perseus died of old age. He had seven children and two daughters: Perses, Alcaeus, Heleus, Mestor, Sthenelus, Electron, Cynurus, Gorgophone (daughter) along with Autochthe (daughter). Perseus' descendants Perseus were the rulers of Mycenae the most powerful town in Peloponnese during Mycenaean time. Heracles (Roman: Hercules) was also a descendant of Perseus. Perses is believed to travel to Asia to be the ancestor of a new race called the Persians.

Theseus

Theseus was the King of Athens most well-known for his killing of (the) Minotaur. He is among the heroes of the attic mythology, such as Perseus, Cadmus, or Hercules. He is also famous for his questionable paternity being the father of Aethra who was the mother of the King Pittheus of Troezen as well as Aegeus the King of Athens and Poseidon god of sea. The myth tells us that a childless Aegeus was in Troezen to solve a problem and was permitted by Pittheus to sleep with Aethra and was advised in a vision in a dream by Athena (daughter of Zeus) to worship Poseidon and did so by pouring libations on Troezen's shores. Poseidon was her savior and she also had a pregnancy gave Theseus immortality and divinity.

Theseus was born in Troezen in the country of his mother and became an extremely brave and wise man. Aegeus left him some tokens when he left the city - tokens made from the (Aegeus) shoes and sword, as proof of his royal lineage. Later, Aethra told Theseus about his father and the kingdom of Athens and advised him the need to return to claim his birthright with the tokens he had already received. In search of excitement The young and courageous Theseus set out to Athens via a treacherous route and came across a number of bandits on the journey.

Theseus was able to complete the Six tasks on his way to Athens.

*He killed Periphetes, the club-wearing bandit at Epidaurus and then took the strong staff that is associated with Theseus until the present day in the form of paintings

*He killed a criminal whose name was Sinis on his home on the Isthmus of Corinth who captured travelers and then decapitated the victims by tying them between two pines, and then let the trees go. Theseus did exactly the same thing to him, and then slept with his daughter who was born Melanippus.

"North" of the Isthmus The killer is an enormous pig called Phaea The Crommyonian Sow.

* In Megara the film, he kills a criminal named Sciron who forced people to clean their feet, and then killed the robbers by throwing them off a cliff as they kneeled.

* Theseus then killed King Cercyon of Eleusis who was a smackdown contestant to anyone who came by to watch a match.

* The final labor was the murder by Procrustes the Stretcher through decapitation.

After arriving in Athens, Theseus discovers his father was married to the sorceress Medea who attempted to murder him by assigning him a mission to eliminate his Marathonian bull. The sorceress then attempted to poison the man after he completed the job. Theseus returns to his father and vows that he will kill Minotaur following that he was fed by the city's citizens Athens as a sacrifice 3 times.

The Minotaur that breathed fire was a half-man half bull monster who was locked up in the Labyrinth as well as fed to the inhabitants in Athens to make an agreement to offer to Minos King of Crete. Theseus had made a promise to the father of his son that, if he came back with a positive result from Crete and was successful, he would raise the white sail in lieu of the black sails of the ship that carried sacrificed people to the Minotaur. However, he did not keep his word and Aegeus committed suicide by throwing himself off a cliff, because the thought that his son had passed away. So, Theseus was made the king of Athens.

Theseus was the one who consolidated the various Attic states into one state with savvy political maneuvering and sheer shrewdness. He also commanded the Athenian army in numerous war campaigns . He is believed to be the founder of Greek democracy. After his demise to the Athenian Assembly, the Athenian was given the chance to take part in numerous adventures. He was acknowledged for being a part of, along alongside Jason as well, as Jason did in Argonautic expeditions as well as in his participation in the Caledonian boar hunt. He also killed the Centaur that abducted his wife when he was drunk at a wedding of a friend's. Legends also say that he was responsible for helping his friend Pirithous in rescuing the goddess' daughter Demeter of the Underworld. Both were caught in the process and were punished by Hades before Hercules was able to come to Theseus to rescue them. As the years passed the adventures caused issues. People became exhausted of the chaos that he created, and when he passed away in exile the people did not take the trouble of bringing his body back to his home.

A variant of the story of his death claims that the man was pushed off an high cliff by Lycomedes, the King of Scyros who failed to stop an uprising backed by Menestheus who was a cousin of one of the former King of Athens. Another story claims that the man was killed accidentally by his wife. He was stained by that of the centaur's blood. Theseus who had earlier saved her from.

Generations passed until Theseus's remains were taken to home by Cimon who was an Athenian general of the war. The burial was in a stunning tomb in Athens which served as refuge for the weak. Theseus festivals, Theseia, was held on the eighth day of the 10th month.

Hercules

Hercules (Heracles in Greek) was the son of Zeus from the mortal woman called "Alcmene" and was the only person who was transformed into a God after his death. He was famous for his determination and strength, however He was not wise. He played an important role in Zeus his rule was overthrown from the giants.

When giants gathered to take on Mount Olympus, they threw several mountains in order to get to Zeus's throne, which was in the clouds. This was Hercules who made use of his tremendous power to pull the mountain range down, which impeded giants from getting into the clouds. This was where Zeus and the other Olympians resided.

As a young man when he was young, he was married to a beautiful woman whom he deeply loved and was blessed with three sons. He killed his own wife after Hera (Goddess of Marriage and Family as well as Hercules stepmother who was jealous) caused him to go insane because she didn't want him to having a good life. But, when Hercules was able to come to terms with his feelings He wanted to commit suicide due to his sorrow. His friend, 'Theseus' has convinced him to come up with a plan to make amends for his sins.

Hercules was sent to Oracle to get advice from Oracle who instructed that he had to complete the twelve jobs which Eurystheus (King of Mycenae) was going to assign the task to him. He followed the instructions Oracle advised and completed the twelve tasks , which seemed impossible for a human being. The twelve tasks included:

The first task given to Hercules was to kill an Nemean lion , which was impervious against any kind of weapon. Hercules killed it using his hands, and then went to finish another task.

The third mission was to take down a monster dubbed "Hydra. He killed the 9-headed monster with the aid by his son Iolaus.

Then, he killed Cerynitian Hind (deer) which was his target to keep alive. This deer is sacred to the goddess Artemis and she wouldn't let Hercules to kill the deer. After hearing about his tale, she decided to let him go.

Then, he went to the place of Centaurs to hunt down the Erymanthian boar. In his attempt to lure the Boar it was attacked by the Centaurs, but the wolf managed to kill a few of them, and the remaining were able to escape. The boar was captured and returned it to Eurystheus.

Then, he cleaned the Augeius's stable in just one day, something that was difficult to accomplish since it would take months for a human to wash it. He was able to accomplish this by dispersing two rivers through the stable to make it completely clean.

The other tasks he carried out included getting rid of his Stymphalian birds away and the bringing of Cretan bulls back to Knossos and returning Mares in Diomedes back as well as the bringing of his Girdle home, and bringing the cattle of Geryon back returning golden apples from Hesperides and the return of the dog that guards Underworld named 'Cerberus.'

In his 11th labor he ran into Prometheus who was bound to a rock as well as a bald eagle eat his liver. He killed the bird and released Prometheus. Apart from the other difficulties that he faced in his travels and adventures, he was constantly confronted with the hate of Hera which caused problems in his life. After his death, Zeus took his immortal half to Olympus and transformed him into god.

We'll learn more about Prometheus next time.

Chapter 6: Prometheus

Prometheus is a Titan God who had a reputation for being a trickster. He was one of the principal Gods who fought to control Heaven among Titans and Olympians that lasted almost 10 years. The pivotal moment of the battle came when Titans were unable to use low-cost tricks in a battle which Prometheus suggested. The result was that he switched his sides to join Zeus.

Zeus utilized the techniques that Prometheus suggested that was the basis as well as break for the fight. Zeus and the Olympians prevailed. Following Titanomachy, Prometheus, Epimetheus (Prometheus' brother) as well as additional Gods received the responsibility of creating humans and other earthly creatures and also giving them gifts to ensure that they would be successful and live long.

This is the way Prometheus created the first man from clay, while other

Gods created all the different creatures of Earth. When the time to distribute gifts camearound, Epimetheus presented gifts to other creatures. The most significant gifts he gave were wings to birds , and fur for mammals. However, when he came to mankind the world, he had nothing.

Prometheus was sorry for humanity's poor and weak condition and when Epimetheus was depleted of his gifts, he donated the power of fire and metalwork as gifts to humanity and guided his followers on how to utilize the gifts.

It's the Gift of Fire & Prometheus" Punishment

Prometheus took over the workshop located on Mount Olympus (ran by Athena and Hephaestus) and took the fire to give it to human beings. He concealed the fire in the hollow of a fennel stalk and gifted the world to assist people in their daily struggle to live.

The act was astonished Zeus and Zeus was punishes Prometheus by dragging Prometheus to Caucasus which was to the east. In the east, Zeus chained him to an unmoving rock. In the next, Zeus also sent an eagle in order to eat his liver. Prometheus which grew every night after the eagle gone.

Each day the eagle would return to feed on the liver of the growing and Prometheus was subject to this inexplicably long sentence of Zeus up to the point that Hercules (a Hero and human benefactor) encountered Prometheus as he walked through. Hercules killed Prometheus using an arrow and released Prometheus from his sentence.

While Zeus punished Prometheus but his fury did not end there. Zeus tried to take revenge on mankind as well through the Pandora's Box.

Chapter 7: Pandora's Box

Zeus was furious at mankind after being given the gift of flame from Prometheus and he pleaded with Hephaestus (God in the form of Craftsmen and Sculptors Fire, Metals and Artisans) to make a woman from the same mix used to create men. Hephaestus created the first woman from clay and gave her the name Pandora. Zeus's motive was to punish man shape of Pandora therefore he requested each God as well as Goddess to bless her with gifts.

According to the decree of Zeus, each God and Goddess presented gifts to Pandora which included gifts of good quality like beauty and music, charm and so on as well as other gifts that could be used to the favor of man or against his. The gifts offered included persuasion, curiosity and so on. Pandora was given to man with a container referred to in the form of Pandora's Box and instructions from Zeus to keep the box closed. box at any time. In some accounts the box is described as a jar, or a container.

Zeus knew that prohibiting Pandora won't stop her from opening the box, but it will just increase her interest in the things kept in that it. He put some vile items in the box to punish humanity, such as illness, hatred, disease and envy, among others. Epimetheus was aware that Zeus was doing something, and he inserted hope into the box, to ensure that Pandora and all humanity remained protected even when horrible events occurred when Pandora opened the box.

One day, her curiosity was arousing and she took the box out. When she lifted the lid evil things vanished and spread across the globe. She immediately slammed it shut but it was too for her to do so. She began to cry over the destruction she caused to humanity. But, when Epimetheus was able to hear her cry, the king of the universe came to her.

Pandora displayed the empty box after lifting the lid. When she opened it more, a bug emerged and smiling at Pandora and sped away. The name of the bug was "hope" and it made an impact on the world after all the bad things disappeared. The legend of Pandora inspired Ancient Greeks believe that all humanity's troubles originated from that Pandora's Box. Today the word Pandora's Box is used to be a reference to being in trouble.

But, it also provided them with optimism. It helped those Greeks think that, if they had faith it could be possible to make things better and that's exactly what makes mankind triumph in the most depressing of times.

Another major story in Greek mythology is the one about "Oedipus as well as the prophecy that self-fulfills. I'll go over this in the next chapter.

Chapter 8: Oedipus And The Self-Fulfilling Prophecy

Self-fulfilling prophecy refers to the prediction of an event to come that takes place by itself, either through indirect or direct means. It is usually because of an incorrect understanding of the situation, and resulting in an entirely new behaviour, which causes the misunderstood scenario to become a reality. It is believed that in Greek Mythology, there are several prophecies of this kind. The tale of Oedipus is among them.

The Story of Oedipus and The Self-Fulfilling Prophecy

The story of Oedipus is told in Greek Mythology, Oedipus was the king who ruled Thebes. Oedipus was the son of Laius who was the ruler of Thebes prior to his reign. He was unaware of his mother's name. Jocasta and had four children with Jocasta. The tale of Oedipus started when Laius sought out the Oracle to determine whether he'd be able to have kids with his partner , 'Jocasta.'

The prophecy was revealed from the Oracle that any son of Laius who was born from mating with Jocasta could kill them. In the course of time, Jocasta got pregnant and gave birth to a baby boy. Laius directed his servants to cut the baby's ankles to prevent him from being in a position to crawl. This is why the baby was named Oedipus meaning 'swollen foot' in Greek.

Jocasta offered Oedipus the shepherd, and demanded that he carry the infant to the mountains and leave him to die. The shepherd then gave Oedipus the attention of another, who brought Oedipus back to Corinth to present him to the King Polybus as well as Queen Merope, who were rulers over Corinth.

They adopted Oedipus and took him in like their child. As he grew older the family member told him the truth that Merope and Polybus were not his biological parents. He decided to look into the matter further, so he visited Oracle to inquire. Then it was revealed that he planned to kill his father, and later get married to his mother.

He believed that the prophecy could be about Merope and Polybus So he chose to stay clear of the prophecy. Instead of heading back to Corinth the next day, he began moving towards Thebes. As he walked, Oedipus came across his real father , 'King Laius who was planning to the Oracle. Oedipus as well as King Laius stopped each other from getting through, and Laius's charioteer began fighting with Oedipus about who should go through first. The argument culminated in a fight, which ended with Oedipus shooting down the Charioteer as well as Laius. In this way, he did not realize he had fulfilled the first part of the prophecy which was to kill his father's biological father.

As he traveled on his way to Thebes, he encountered Sphinx who was a monster that was plagued by Thebes with its destructive wrath, and killing those who did not be able to answer the questions. Sphinx asked Oedipus to answer a question, and then told Oedipus that he could live if he could answer the question correctly.

It was a question: "What is the name of the creature who walks with four feet every morning and 2 feet during the day,, and 3 feet in the evening?" Oedipus gave the right answer after having the time of his life. He informed Sphinx that it was the man who crawls on four feet when he's in the child stage, then is able to walk on 2 feet once mature and requires sticks when he's old, hence walking on three feet. Sphinx was killed when she fell off the rock on which she was sitting because she was not in a position to accept that her puzzle was correctly answered.

Oedipus was taken to Thebes in Thebes, where Creon was in charge following the death of Laius. Creon was the younger brother of Jocasta and had declared that whoever killed

Sphinx was to be made King and marry Jocasta. When he learned that Oedipus killed Sphinx and was greeted by his victim with honor and offered his sister's hand, and the kingdom as well.

Oedipus accepted his responsibility with dignity and aplomb. He also married his mother in secret and was ruled by Thebes for a period of period of. Thus, he fulfilled the second portion of his prophecy when he married his mother's biological daughter.

A few years later, a plague was ravaging The city of Thebes and Oedipus requested that 'Creon' consult with Oracle. Oracle informed Creon that all of this happened because Laius' killer hadn't been found guilty. Oedipus sought out the prophet (Tiresias) to identify the murderer of Laius. Tiresias informed him the truth that Oedipus that it was Oedipus himself who had killed Laius as well as the fact that he isn't sure the identity of his parents. Creon and Oedipus began to fight at the moment. Jocasta intervened and told him about her son's tale, who she believes died.

In the midst of all that the messenger from Corinth was summoned to the court and informed everyone, including Oedipus that Polybus was dead. Oedipus was relieved at hearing the passing of his father because he believed that he could have avoided the first part in his prophecy. However, he was unable to attend Polybus' funeral Polybus so as to avoid meeting her mother, and thus committing to the second part of his prophecy.

The messenger informed Oedipus to him it was true that Merope and Polybus were not his actual parents Oedipus along with everyone in the court realized Oedipus had killed his real father and then married his actual mother. Jocasta left the courthouse and took her own life through hanging.

Oedipus was able to take a brooch out of his mother's dress and blinded himself by poking his eyes by rubbing the brooch. After that, he fled Thebes with the aid of his daughter. They eventually finally reached Athens in the city of Athens, where both were received with a royal welcome by the King Theseus. He passed away in Athens after a time.

The reign of gods and goddesses was marked by numerous battles which had a major impact on the events that took place. Let's now look at some of the major battles in mythology. Let us also examine what we can learn from the Trojan War in detail, since it is among the most significant battles in the whole of Greek mythology.

Chapter 9: The Battles

The Greek Mythology is full of combats that took place at times. The list is long, but there are some that deserve inclusion in this book. The battles that are mentioned include: The Lelantine War (war between Eretria and Chalkis) The Messenian War (war between Dorians and Spartans) and the Battle in Marathon (War Between Athenians and Persians).

But, the most significant one is Titanomachy (War Between Olympian Titan Gods) and Titan Gods) and the Trojan War. Since I've already discussed Titanomachy and the Trojan War, I'll go over this Trojan War here.

The Trojan War

The Trojan War that happened between Achaeans (Greeks) and Troy as a city Troy is the single most significant moment of Greek Mythology. It was the time Zeus believed that the population of Earth was increasing too much, and he decided to reduce the number of people. The other reason was to rid himself of his godchildren who were very numerous because he had numerous affairs in mortal relationships.

War is the Reason for War

Zeus loved Thetis (Sea Nymph) but he was aware of a prophecy stating that Thetis will be the mother of an unborn son who will be more godlike that his father. Another prophecy Zeus thought of was one that his mother gave him "He will be snatched off the throne by one the sons of his." To prevent both prophecies being fulfilled He devised a plan to solve his whole problem by a simple solution. He decided to give up Thetis and got married to the King Peleus.

To celebrate the union between Thetis as well as Peleus, Zeus threw a lavish dinner which was attended by all Gods and other significant characters, including Eris (Goddess of Strife) who was held at the entrance, which made her angry. She then threw her prize (Apple Of Discord) to the guests before she left. The golden apple contained written on it words which read "to the most beautiful". The debate over the purchase of the apple turned into a dispute between the three Goddesses; Athena, Hera and Aphrodite. The three goddesses were able to turn towards Zeus and demanded him to solve the issue.

Zeus recognized that he was unable to make a choice on behalf of just one Goddess because it could cause the other two to oppose him , which is why he requested Paris (Prince of Troy) to be his judge. If Paris was unable to determine the fate of the apple after he had seen the three Goddesses naked and naked, the Goddesses were able to lure him. Particularly, Athena started by offering the greatest wisdom and battle capabilities. Aphrodite then offered her Helen as the world's most gorgeous woman. Hera gave him the opportunity to be the ruler of Asia. Paris accepted the offer of Aphrodite returning to Troy.

In the meantime, a number of suitors showed up in the courts of Tyndareus (King of Sparta and Helen's father) and demanded Helen's hand to marry. In the midst of Tyndareus' hesitation to decide one suitor , 'Odysseus provided assistance, however, he also asked Penelope's hand to marry, to which Tyndareus complied. Odysseus advised that all suitors sign an oath to safeguard the bride and groom prior to Tyndareus selects Helen's husband. Everyone was in agreement and took the oath , and following that, Tyndareus selected Menelaus as Helen's husband.

Menelaus was married to Helen and was crowned He was the king of Sparta. In the meantime, Aphrodite had to keep her vow she made to Paris which is why she sent Paris to a diplomatic mission to Sparta while Menelaus went away to be buried by his uncle in Crete. Helen was delighted to receive him and within a flash of her eye, became infatuated with the love with the young Trojan prince. The two lovers parted ways to Troy just before the arrival of Menelaus.

When Menelaus returned from Crete when he returned from Crete, he discovered that his wife was missing. He was able to take Odysseus and headed to Troy to retrieve his wife. However, all of his attempts to negotiate did not succeed. He sought out his brother Agamemnon for help and asked all Achaean leaders to honor their pledge to protect Helen as well as himself. Prior to going to war, Menelaus also was able to have Achilles (Son of Thetis) to his side with the aid of Odysseus Phoenix, Ajax and Telamonjan. The addition of Achilles was deemed necessary at the time, since there was an ancient prophecy that Troy would only fall into the hand of Achilles.

8. Year Extension

With Achilles at their side, Achaean leaders assembled at the port of Aulis. Prior to going to war they offered a sacrifice for Apollo and saw a serpent that appeared on the altar, and ate an ostrich and its nine children, and then changed into stone. A seer named Calchas observed the scene as a sign of the times and predicted Troy would fall, but only in the 10th years of war. However, that did not dampen the Achaeans morale even as they set off to Troy.

But, no one was aware of the route to Troy and they ended up at Mysia which was a city that was ruled by the king Telephus. When Telephus saw a ship approaching and he fought it out however, at the same time there was a storm that caused chaos to his Achaean fleet. But, Telephus got injured in battle by the wrath by Achilles as his injuries didn't be healed.

He sought out an Oracle who said that only Achilles could treat his wounds. So, he confronted Achilles however Achilles said that he was ignorant of the art of healing. Odysseus recommended that Achilles spear could help heal Telephus's wound. So, Telephus took the iron from Achilles spear to heal his wound.

In exchange for the help provided in exchange for help from Odysseus and Achilles Telephus was able to show them the path to Troy. But in lieu of continuing the journey they returned home , as the majority of their fleets had been scattered due to a storm that struck the sea. This event put an end to the Trojan War for the next eight years.

The Siege of 10 Years as well as Achaean' Victory

Eight years later, Achaean leadership gathered again in the harbor of Aulis to set off towards Troy. On their way they stopped on The island of Tenedos and, from there, they sent a mission of diplomatic service to Troy which was to petition the Trojan King to bring back Helen but was denied at the gates of Troy. Then the Greek fleets set sail to the end of the journey.

The moment the Greek fleet arrived at Troy the Greeks were wary to step foot on Trojan soil as the prophecy was saying that those who set foot on Trojan ground first was the one one to be killed in combat. But, Odysseus found the courage and dropped his shield onto the ground before stepping on the ground. Protesilaus continued to follow him, but not with the shield that didn't go well for him since He was the first person to die in battle at the at the hands of Hector (Trojan Prince).

The entire fleet arrived in Troy, Greeks laid a siege over Troy which lasted for nine years. The siege was not completely over because Troy was able to continue commerce between Asian cities and receive reinforcements, too. In the course of nine long years during which the Achaean army wanted to go back home, but Achilles got them to stay.

The tenth year was when Agamemnon made Achilles's mistress his own. This resulted in Achilles angry and refused to fight, and stayed inside his camp. As the Achaeans continued to fight without Achilles and they suffered several losses which led Patroclus (Achilles his close friend) to assume the command of Achilles's Myrmidon army. While leading the army into combat, he was shot in battle by Hector (Trojan prince) who had superior battle capabilities. When Achilles received the news the news, he was angry and declared vengeance over the death of his friend. Agamemnon Also sent Achilles his lover back which led to the two leaders reuniting and they were able to agree to fight yet again.

After Achilles returned to his troops and returned to the battle, the Achaeans once again triumphant. Achilles was killed by Hector as well, and refused to take his body back to be buried. He sewed the body of Hector to the rear of his chariot before dragging it away from the walls of Troy. When the Trojan King begged for the body of his son, Achilles returned it to him for an appropriate burial.

Then, Achilles was killed by an arrow poisonous that was fired by Paris and struck Achilles' heel. Paris was also killed in the fight. The tenth year was when Odysseus created an idea to win the war. He commanded his troops to build a horse made of wood which was hollow inside. Once the horse was complete the horse was taken into the town gates, and was left there as a present from Achaeans.

The entire Achaean soldiers appeared to be leaving the ground, but a lot of them were still inside the horse. When Trojan was able to see Greeks departing, they rejoiced because they felt that they had taken the victory. They took the horse into the city and began to celebrate. As the Trojan soldiers became drunk they were surrounded by Greeks emerged from their horse to kill the drunk soldiers. The battle continued until eventually the Greeks were able to take over Troy.

Greeks were unmerciful and smashed the city to pieces and even destroyed temples, which offended a lot of Gods. A majority of the soldiers did not return since they had upset their Gods. Zeus's scheme worked, in the end, as it was the Trojan War resulted in thousands dead, including many gods.

While this chapter covers one important aspect of mythology, I have yet to provide insight into the most important aspectthe myth of The Odyssey. The final chapter deals with that.

Chapter 10: The Odyssey

The poem was composed sometime around 700 BC the epic "Odyssey," written in the 700 BC, is one of the first as well as longest epics. Epic is a lengthy poem that is derived from myths and ancient traditions and recounts the adventures of heroes or legends from a specific country or.

The Odyssey composed by Homer is a story of Odysseus who is the King of Ithaca who has been absent from his home and his family for the past 20 years. The poem is spread across 24 books, and each provides a new sequence of events that were experienced by Odysseus. Although it's impossible to explain the epic in full detail in this book, here's an overview of the poem that provides an outline of the Odyssey is all about.

The Overview of The Odyssey

Odysseus was most well-known during the war due to his role in the creation of The Trojan horse, which was a massive wooden horse which was thought as a present to the Trojans from the in retreating Greeks. The Trojans were delighted to receive the gift and began to celebrate the gift. As night fell and everyone was drinking when it was the Greek fighters who were concealed themselves in the body hollow of the horse came out and killed the Trojans and won the war.

Following the conclusion of the Trojan War, Odysseus made an ten-year trip between Troy to Ithaca which was his home. The journey of Odysseus is chronicled chronologically in this manner:

* Storms brought Odysseus ship on a journey to Cyclops Polyphemus. He began feeding on the crews and the ship. Odysseus was able to fool Polyphemus and, with his friends, blinded the Cyclops. When they left Odysseus made the mistake of revealing his identity Polyphemus. He then revealed his identity to his father about the god

Poseidon. Poseidon decides to take on his son's revenge against him. He causes a storm in the sea to destroy Odysseus However, Athena helps him and saves the man.

They then arrived at an island inhabited by the god of wind, Aeolus, who put all winds with the exception of the west wind into bag and handed that bag Odysseus. The west winds blew through the ships to Ithaca. Just before they got to the shoreline, Odysseus' companions took the bag of wind from Odysseus believing it was gold, they opened it up and let out all the winds. The ships were blown from the island and returned to where they began. Aeolus was not willing helping them once more and so they quit.

* They visited their destination, the Island of the Laestrygonians, an animalistic tribe that devoured every member of the crew but not the one of Odysseus his ship. They quickly left the island , and got to the island of the witch Circe. Circe transformed Odysseus's group of companions into

pigs. Odysseus who was gifted a magical herb from Hermes who was Hermes's son, refused to believe her magic. Circe became infatuated with Odysseus and changed the pigs back into human beings. After staying there for just one year and then left to go on their journey

* On the island known as Thrinacia, Odysseus had caught the cattle of the sun god Helios. Helios furious, he demanded that Zeus take them to the cross or else he'd let the sun sparkle throughout the Underworld. Zeus obliged and caused the ship to sink, and only Odysseus was able to escape. Odysseus landed on the island Ogygia and was greeted by the witch Calypso held him for seven years due to the fact that her love for him was a secret until Hermes intervened to free the hero. Odysseus was then able to reach an island belonging to the Phaeacians (the contemporary Island of Corfu) which was the place where he received help to him to reach his destination.

While in Ithaca there was a massive crowd of suitors was constantly dissuaded Penelope Odysseus's spouse to get married. They had encroached on the palace of Odysseus and demolished his property. Even though they were cruel, Penelope remains faithful to Odysseus and waits for his return.

Telemachus is Odysseus's son. He is determined to take on the men who are pursuing him, but he is powerless to stop the suitors. Many believe Odysseus has died, he's actually alive and is being held from Calypso the nymph that fell in love with the man. The gods and goddesses of the various gods of Mount Olympus debate on whether they should help Odysseus. Athena ultimately decides to save Odysseus by helping Telemachus.

In disguise, she appears to be an acquaintance to Laertes the Telemachus's grandpa as she convinces Telemachus to convene an assembly to fight the lovers. Athena also helps prepare Telemachus for a trip towards Sparta along with Tylos. After reaching the two places, Telemachus meets Menelaus and Nestor who are the friends of Odysseus whom inform Telemachus that his father is alive and imprisoned in Calypso's island.

Telemachus is planning to save his father, but before that Telemachus decides to head back home to meet his mother. In Ithaca The suspects are planning to kill and ambush Telemachus. At this point, the Zeus called Hermes and asked Hermes to aid Odysseus escape Calypso. In the end, he succeeds in convincing Calypso to release Odysseus.

Ithaca

Then, Odysseus returned to his home, but was disguised as a begging man by Athena. He lost everything he had earned in gold as well as wealth gained during his time in the Trojan War. He confesses himself to Telemachus but requests him to remain silent until he has defeated the potential suitors. Odysseus is treated badly and mocked by his suitors in his home, and is particularly vilified by an obscene man called Antinous. A housekeeper named Eurycleia finds out the identity of Odysseus when she spots an old scar while she washes his feet. Eurycleia is trying to inform Penelope concerning the beggar's identity however Athena assures her that Penelope does not hear her. Odysseus vows Eurycleia to remain silent. Odysseus' dog , who was a young puppy when it went on a trip to Trojan war was able to recognize the dog and was so excited that he passed away. The incident was witnessed by Penelope caused her to believe that the person who begged was Odysseus.

The Slaying of the Suitors

In order to determine her suspicions to determine her suspicions, she holds an archery tournament and declares that she will get married to that man carry Odysseus's bow and shoot an archer through 12 axes, the most famous feat Odysseus has achieved to date.

The suitors all participate in the contest , but are unsuccessful in winning. Then Odysseus dressed as beggar takes the stage and wins the contest. He takes an arrow and shoots through Antinous his head first. Odyssey is aided by the aid by Telemachus, his brother Telemachus and the other men he had joined and killed all suitors with arrows, shooting at them, and later with spears and swords after both sides have prepared themselves. After the battle is over, Odysseus and Telemachus hang twelve house maids who Eurycleia suspects of having betrayed Penelope or having sexual relations with the suitors or both. They also slaughter and dismember the goatherd Melanthius who ridiculed and abhorred Odysseus and brought arms and weapons to suitors. The men reveal who he is to Penelope. He is reluctant, but she is able to recognize him after he says that he constructed their bed out of an olive tree which was still planted into the soil. Many scholars believe that this could be the end of the Odyssey and the remainder is an interpolation.

The Final

The following day Odysseus, Telemachus, and Penelope eventually join with Odysseus's father Laertes, who also accepts his name only after Odysseus accurately describes the orchard Laertes had earlier given to him. They are snatched from the relatives of lovers Odysseus had killed, as well as those of his family members who were Ithaca sailors who went with the king to Troy. Zeus demands Athena to intervene to restore peace in the area. The long and difficult ordeal of Odysseus comes to an end.

Chapter 11: the Seeds of Strife

Zeus Lord of Zeus, Lord of the Olympian Gods and the son of Titan Chronos and the 3rd generation celestial creatures that inhabited the universe, was always on the move. His fights with his father's kin to supremacy in the cosmos allowed him to form an entire race of human beings unmatched in their intelligence and hard work and he longed for to create a stage where the most talented of humankind could test their skills.

Capricious and erratic, Zeus soon found an occasion to test his most beloved creation, while also preventing his own death. His father Chronos had eaten all his children to stop from fulfilling a prediction in which one could overthrow him. However, Zeus was clever enough to not be consumed and bring the prophecy to fulfillment. Of of course, Zeus was not inclined to allow the same to occur to his own children. After hearing that one his own children Metis could overthrow him, Zeus swallowed his entire mother during her pregnancy so that the children wouldn't have a birth to Metis instead of to Zeus. But a second prophecy about his demise was revealed about a child of the latest subject of his lust which is The sea Nymph Thetis.

Zeus was not a person who is likely to let a prophecy sabotage his romantic desires, however in the instance of Thetis she chose to forgo his usual prudence and made a decision to marry her to the old Peleus, the king of Aegina. Peleus who was from Aegina. Zeus organized a wonderful wedding for the couple in Aegina and also invited all the gods - the whole lot with the exception of Eris who was the goddess of conflict and conflict.

Zeus's gaze then focused on The city of Sparta as well as the Queen who resided there. Queen Leda was known as beautiful and generosity, and which is why Zeus appeared from Olympus to her disguised as an eagle-like swan that was fleeing from a dangerous Eagle. Leda was captivated by the beauty and beauty of the swan, and then eventually swam in it, fulfilling Zeus's love. In the next few days, Leda gave birth to two eggs. As she had been sleeping with her husband the very night that she laid her eggs with the swan, there was not a way to determine which egg had immortal or divine offspring. however when two sisters and two brothers were born, Leda and Tyndareus adopted the entire family with joy. Kastor and Polydeuces are called the Dioskouroi were the twins born to Leda and Tyndareus. Their exploits ultimately earned them a spot in heaven. But the sister of their father Helen who is often referred as the prettiest woman on earth that fueled the mythology surrounding that of the Trojan War.

A fable from the past depicting Menelaus and Helen

As Helen reached maturity, the most renowned heroes of Greece went to Sparta in order to get her hand at the hands of King Tyndareus. Princes and kings alike fought for her love and that of her father, who was ultimately the one to make the choice. But the king Tyndareus did not take pride or joy in the affection that his child received from these gentlemen and, in actual fact, was shocked by it.

In all of the men, these kings princes and heroes were the most easily offended, and were the most likely to join forces and attack the city due to their discontent over the outcome of the battle to win Helen's hand. The greatest heroes, like Ajax, Diomedes, Menestheus and the clever Odysseus who sat in the royal court and became more and more agitated during his uncertainty. Odysseus although certainly drawn to Helen but was attracted by the beauty and intellect of Penelope who was the child of Icarius. Conscient of how much threat Sparta faced, Odysseus approached King Tyndareus and suggested an alternative: if Tyndareus would back his suit for Penelope, Odysseus would obtain the oath of all the Helen's lovers to accept the decision of Tyndareus without bloodshed, and to defend his marriage to Helen to the person her father chooses. In recognition of the ability Odysseus was to become well-known for, the king agreed to his offer.

A Roman bust depicting Odysseus

Menelaus is the cousin of the king Agamemnon of Mycenae and a great prince of his own but was less open about his love for Helen, the Spartan princess. So, he pleaded with his brother to travel to Sparta in his place and try to win Helen's affections and offered the sacrifice of 100 oxen for Aphrodite should he get Helen's hand.

When the time was right to take a decision Tyndareus gave the prince who was absent Menelaus. After the news reached Mycenae, Menelaus travelled to Sparta immediately to wed the gorgeous
Helen. Tyndareus's days are now over and shortly Menelaus would be ascending onto the throne in Sparta with his newlywed wife at his side.

But, amid the excitement of his success, Menelaus made the gravest mistake of his life. He failed to keep his promise to Aphrodite. In actual fact, Zeus had depended on this error. However, Eris, ignorant of Zeus's deeds, took deep offrage at being ignored by the gods at their ceremonies. Before she marched towards the marriage to challenge Zeus regarding the issue Eris first created the gift of discord to the immortals around her intended to punish and remind everyone about her name. As she arrived at the entrance to the hall for the wedding at the direction of the goddess messenger Hermes who informed Eris that Zeus had instructed that he not to let her in at any time. Eris didn't dispute the decision with Hermes however, she let her hand fall a golden apple out of her hands and left. The apple was tossed through Hermes and into the room in which the wedding was being held and landed in the space between gods Hera, Athena, and Aphrodite.

The apple sparkled from the floor and attracted the attention of everyone on the day of the ceremony. Its skin was engraved with "For the Most Beautiful," as well as the goddesses who were equally in appearance and beauty each claimed it was hers. The three goddesses had a great debate. the three goddesses, who were capable of shredding the world apart in their confidence. Zeus was able to stand between his daughters and wife and explained to them that he was aware of a fair and impartial person who had proved that he was an impartial justice in past cases. He could bring peace to their dispute.

The result was that Hermes took the three goddesses on the isle of Ida which was where the young herdsman Paris lived. Paris was exiled out of the palace of Troy because a prophecy predicted that he would be the ruination of the city should he continued to live. "The the first child born to Hecuba was Hector who was an additional baby was about to be born, Hecuba believed that she had created a firebrand and the fire was able to spread across the entire city, and then burned it. When Priam was informed of the dream of Hecuba she had, he contacted his son Aesacus to be examined, as he was a dream interpreter as trained by his father's mother Merops. He said that the child was destined to destroy his country , and recommended to be exposed."[1[1

An ancient Roman statue depicting Paris

When the goddesses arrived they were bathed within the River Ida and presented themselves before Paris in their stunning naked beauty. Paris was awed by the stunning beauty of the three goddesses, stated that he could not decide between the three goddesses. Dissuaded but not defeated, the three gods came to this young person and immediately began to offer him rewards that were beyond the most arduous of desires. Hera came to Paris and offered him power in politics and complete control over Europe in addition to Asia. Athena followed her to Paris and informed him that she would give him the wisdom, experience and skill of battle and the skills of the greatest warriors , living and dead. Then Aphrodite was as light and sensual as an asp was seen walking towards Paris and whispered to his the ear of the man: "If you present the apple to me, I'll offer you the admiration of the most gorgeous woman on earth."

"The Judgment of Paris" by the author Enrique Simonet "The The Judgment Of Paris"

Paris knew of Helen and Achaeans, just as many Achaeans, as well as non-Achaeans, had been, and was aware as Aphrodite her marriage to Menelaus. But, Paris trusted the goddess of love to honor her vow, and handed the golden apple into her hands. Zeus smiled at Aphrodite while she exacted revenge on Menelaus in the knowledge that many would be subject to the wrath of Hera and Athena in the near future.

While back in the Palace in Sparta, Menelaus enjoyed his newly-acquired title as king and wife to the most gorgeous woman of all time. He was elated in the way only a king unaware of his deeds could. When he heard that an unnamed Trojan was arriving in his port and was waiting to be welcomed for dinner in the palace. "For nine days, he enjoyed the company of Menelaus however, on the 10th day Menelaus going to Crete to conduct the obsequies of his father's mother Catreus, (Paris) persuaded Helen to travel with him."[2[2

Many have accused Helen of being a shrewd nymph or being a harlot, but the careful servant or slave in the Menelaus's room the night Paris entered might have been able to hear the sound of Eros' bowstring when he shot Helen through the heart , according to Aphrodite's instructions. On the other hand, Paris was young and reckless and believed that the divine blessing bestowed on him by Aphrodite will not bring any consequences for his abduction of Helen. He floated off into night as if he had the support of all gods, however Paris would soon realize that the blessings of one god did not mean the favor of all.

Paintings by Francesco Primaticcio
"The The Abduction of Helen"

Chapter 12: Heading to War

The moment Menelaus came back to Sparta and found that Helen was missing, he went into a fit of rage. His employees informed him that the prince from Troy was the one who had taken her away and immediately pleaded with his wise friend Odysseus go with his to Troy to ask for her to return. But, upon arriving at Troy the Trojans advised they had numerous precedents against returning captives, for instance, abduction of Medea from another Achaean. Thus it was decided that the Trojans did not allow her to be released.

After being rejected by the court, the couple were able to return to Greece and began to invoke the holy oath which Helen's lovers had taken to King Tyndareus. "He was at Agamemnon at Mycenae and pleaded with him to form an army to fight Troy and to increase levies in Greece. Then he sent an edict to each of the kings made them aware of the oaths they had swornto, and warned them to pay attention at the safety of their wives in announcing that the affront was equally dealt with to all Greece."[44

The most powerful Achaean warriors gathered from the far-off cities of Greece to commemorate the oath that they had taken. Agamemnon acknowledged them all and Menelaus thanked them all before the brothers issued the command to each commander on his ship to sail towards Troy.

While en route to the magnificent citadel However everyone was afflicted by storms. Ships smashed into rocks and they nearly lost their routes in the troughs before they could find a safe harbor. Calchas Seer Calchas, a renowned seer, told the captains that they were suffering from the storms that were brought on by Artemis due to the fact that Agamemnon killed a deer that was sacred to her. The Achaeans were unsure of what to do to please the goddess. Calchas advised his followers the following: Agamemnon had to sacrifice his child, Iphigenia.

At this point, Agamemnon saw the war with Troy as an opportunity for him to immortalize his story among all the legendary Achaean heroes. Afraid of war and hungry for battle Agamemnon was king. Agamemnon battled off his paternal resentments and pleaded with his daughter. Artemis was pity for this innocent child, bound her up as an animal sacrifice and- seeing the ferocity of the growing war, flew down and substituted Iphigenia with the lamb. "After the offering to Apollo the god of war, a serpent flew off the altar, right next to the plane-tree next to it, the nest was that was devoured by the eight sparrows that were in the nest, along with the mother bird, who created 9th, transformed into stone. Calchas claimed that the signification was given to them by the Will of Zeus He was able to conclude from the event that Troy was meant to be taken over 10 years."[5[5]

In spite of the prophecy from Zeus, Zeus' prophecy was not fulfilled. Achaean commanders were required to honor the oath they took to King Tyndareus which is why they went on towards Troy. As they approached their destination in the Trojan region, Menelaus pleaded his fleet to be stopped at the island nearby of Tenedos in hopes of coming to a conclusion with Trojan King Priam. The embassy's response and the embassy was the same as previously but this time The council of Trojans threatened to execute both Menelaus and Odysseus should they return.

The embassy was still in Troy the troops were discontented. Achilles the boy who was who was born to Thetis and Peleus following the tragic wedding in Aegina was 15 years old and was already proving to be more proficient than the majority of Achaean soldiers who were twice his age, not to mention his fellow soldier Patroclus.

Achilles's inclusion in Agamemnon's mighty army was not a mistake It was his destiny. Zeus wasn't the only immortal to realize that he was committing Thetis in a marriage that was unjust. Young and eternally young, Thetis did not have a desire for the aging Peleus and complied with the dictates from Zeus and soon had an infant. As a demigod infant Achilles was mortal, and in addition, Thetis saw in his future a path that was forked. The choice was either he'd enjoy a long, peaceful life, only to die at an the aging process, or decide to join the ranks and become the most formidable warrior ever to live immortalizing his name through poetry and song forever. In awe of the possibility, Thetis sneaked down to the deadly River Styx and, holding her infant by the heel and then dipped him into the river, creating a young body invulnerable to injury.

Peter Paul Rubens' painting "Thetis Dipping the infant Achilles in the River Styx"

Like all heroes However Achilles was a youthful Achilles was cursed by prophecies that hung over his name. Calchas, just before the fleet left towards Troy demanded Agamemnon to go to Aegina to recruit the boy, but without him the plan was likely to be unsuccessful. The island that was Tenedos However, it was there where Achilles secured his fate. "They affirm that Achilles was firmly commanded with the responsibility by Thetis his mother to not murder Tenes because she was greatly revered by Apollo and that the Goddess made a promise on one of his servants in the household to take extra care and keep him in the consciousness of the situation, in case Achilles would murder Tenes in the midst of the night. When Achilles began to enter Tenedos and was pursued by Tenes's sister Tenes and was very sincere, Tenes met him and stood up for his sister. Eventually, she ran away and fled, but Tenes was killed. Achilles knew that was lying dead, killed his own servant because the presence of Achilles did not advise Achilles to be contrary."[66

The Achaeans were able to observe the formidable citadel, Calchas got another omen of the fact that the very first Greek to arrive in Troy was also the first one to die. Odysseus determined to prove his bravery and fervor for taking on Troy pay for his actions, Trojans pay for the actions of Paris and actions, jumped from his ship when it arrived at the beach, and he handed over his sword to the approaching guards. The Achaeans were impressed by Odysseus's bravery and joined him in a mass. Protesilaus was the first to arrive on the beach, however -after killing a handful of Trojans and a few Trojans, he was met with his end in the fate by Prince Hector. Hector was the prince of Achaean. Achaean army soon discovered that Odysseus did not suffer the fate predicted by Calchas by lowering his shield in front of him on the sandy beach.

A tense battle ensued, during which the Trojans surrendered beaches to invaders and the Greeks constructed a defensive wall and reassessed their supplies. If the gods had decreed that their rule over the Trojan beach would endure for ten years of bloody battle it was inevitable that they waited.

Nine years passed and the Achaeans were incapable of capturing the city, began protecting their territory and cultivating wherever they could and then robbing their adversaries as often as they could. In the realm of larceny, two Achaeans outperformed the other. Ajax The Great was particularly adept at pillaging, and Achilles as it was reported that he robbed 12 islands and 11 cities that were allied with Achilles and the Trojan cause.

A classic representation of Ajax

Marie Lan-Nguyen's illustration of 5th century BCE illustration of Achilles and Ajax playing dice

In these cities, two ladies of extraordinary beauty discovered themselves among the riches. Achilles loved the gorgeous Briseis and Agamemnon was given Chryseis who was the sister of the priest Apollo Chryses as their share.

"Upon the altar of Chryses who was the son of Atreus [Agamemnon] had brought disgrace. He had travelled to the fast ships of Achaeans to save his daughter carrying ransom that was beyond counting and with his hands, were the wreaths of Apollo who strikes from afar, with an gold staff and implored the Achaeans all over and, most importantly, Atreus's two sons Atreus as well as the marshallers of the people: Sons of Atreus and the other well-greaved Achaeans the gods who have homes on Olympus will grant you the right to take over the town of Priam and then return safely to your home; however, my beloved child, release to me, and take the ransom in reverence for the god of Zeus, Apollo who strikes from far away.'

"Then the rest of the Achaeans were astonished, and they all screamed to honor the priest and pay the glorious ransom, but it did not please those who loved Agamemnon the son of Atreus however Agamemnon sent him off with a harsh sentence. "[7]

A illustration of Chryses appealing to Agamemnon to save his daughter.

The general from his Greek military, while Achaeans as well as the Trojans alike were shocked by his indignation. Chryses in a state of shock, demanded Apollo to punish him for his inhumane treatment at the at the hands of Agamemnon and the gods heard his plea. The skies were filled with arrows over that of the Achaean camp, however they weren't made by Trojan hands. The furious god began by attacking the mules, animals as well as the hunting dogs. He then unleashed his divine arrows at the men, bringing a famine for all. In the end, Agamemnon had no choice but to send Chryseis to her father.

The Achaean leader had learned to not be angry with Apollo However, the Achaean leader was not willing for returning to his post empty handed. The soldiers got their portion, and Agamemnon's was the biggest of all -- more even than that of matured Achilles who was the prize that was the son of Atreus was awed by. This was not a game of skills However, Agamemnon was not required to show his worth against Achilles. He was the leader of Achilles' Achaean forces. Any reward was his to be had and he seized the prize he believed was his. Achilles was so angry watching Odysseus leave from the scene with Briseis and Briseis that he called for that neither him as well as any of the Myrmidons who were under his control would ever fight an unworthy leader. He also pleaded with His mother Thetis to visit Zeus and ask him to inflict a calamity on the Greeks to help them realize the error in their leader's conduct and ask for the return of their most formidable warrior. Thetis saw her son's distress and left for Mount Olympus to speak with Zeus, the Lord of Gods.

Zeus who was aware that they were in the ominous 10-year anniversary of the plan sent a vision to Agamemnon. The dream told Agamemnon that Zeus advised him that the gods of Olympus did not have a split in their support for soldiers; they all stood with the Achaeans and Agamemnon was to gather his forces and take on the citadel in a speedy manner. However, before doing this the commander who was arrogant determined to gauge the mood of his soldiers. He wanted to make sure that they believed in him just as much as the gods, and so he advised his troops to leave the country of Troy to their home. He informed the soldiers that their battle was done and they could return home to their families and wives and children, which the Greek troops welcomed with a smile. They started loading their ships and preparing their departure, until Hera angered by her husband's conduct, made an appeal to Athena. The two people who were the victims of Paris's verdict were in a state of shock at the ruling at the time, and Athena responded to Hera's request and walked down from the heights of Olympus to meet Odysseus who was down on the beach, apathetically. "Son of Laertes who was sprung out of Zeus, Odysseus of many illusions, is it in fact that you will throw yourself onto your benchesed ships and escape to your beloved native homeland? And ye will let Priam as well as the Trojans their boasts, or even Argive Helen and her family, for whose for the sake of many an Achaean has perished in Troy away from his home country. However, now go through the Achaeans' host and restrain yourself from now on; and with gentle words try to restrain each one of them from letting them drag into the ocean their curved vessels. "[8]

Odysseus was arousing as he ran along the shore and scolding his fellow countrymen when they loaded up their possessions. He lashed out at their pity as well as their lack of self-confidence and warned the princes and kings of the oaths they'd taken before the gods on the day they were killed in Sparta. A majority of Greeks were convinced by his logic and they soon forced to fight again.

The princes of Troy were able to deploy their forces and were leaving the citadel Hector looked at his brother, the person who brought 10 years of grief to his fellow countrymen and told him to stop doing all he could to protect his people from more bloodshed. Paris realized and was shamed to put himself at the front of the Trojan troops and calling for Menelaus. He demanded Menelaus to win the war with a one-on-1 battle. The cuckolded

King agreed and both pulled their

arms.

"Hector warns Paris for its softness and Advizes Paris to Go to War" by J.H.W. Tischbein

The two armies sat in awe as the prince and the king began to approach at first, and it was an unbalanced battle. Menelaus who was the stronger warrior and king, sent Paris down to the floor repeatedly. The cunning Aphrodite stood on Mount Olympus as her champion was battered to the ground repeatedly. She knew what would happen to Paris should he continue to stand before Menelaus's sword. She went to the battlefield, and swept away before Menelaus was able to deliver the fatal strike.

The forces sat in awe in awe at the events that took place in front of their eyes. However, while mortals were frozen to a state of numbness The immortals were furious over Aphrodite's boldness. Hera ran to her husband, and angry she demanded that he make amends for her actions. Zeus was aware of the grievances of his wife and intervened. Pandarus was an Trojan archer on the frontline, stood with an arrow in his fingers in a tense state, waiting for the commander's message to let him know the duel-truce was lifted. But, thanks to Zeus his grip was loosening and one arrow was released from the Trojan troops. The arrow pierced the skin of the leg of Menelaus and broke the peace between the forces. The two armies attacked.

Zeus's heroes fulfilled his wish and, in the midst of the battle they achieved their full bloodthirsty capacity. Diomedes caused a massacre of the Trojan army. They fell in large numbers upon his horse, which included the unlucky Pandarus and his companion Aeneas who was the his son from the prince crippled Anchises. Anchises was once an elegant and brave prince, so so in the sense that Aphrodite was adamant to lay beside him. After the fool prince boasted about his achievements Aphrodite, her goddess of love slayed his son in retaliation. However, as their son was set to fall victim to his sword Diomedes, Aphrodite descended upon the battlefield to help one of her favorite soldiers.

The painting of William Blake Richmond depicts Aphrodite and Anchises

Diomedes was furious. Any thoughts of cosmological significance and all sentiments of pious obeisance were torn apart in his fury. the hero remembered the prayer which was answered by Athena in the battle. "Wherefore when any god should arrive to make a trial of you, do not you ever fight in a face-to-face battle with any gods of the immortal realm and only when Aphrodite is the daughter of Zeus is to enter the fray, and her you smite her with a thrust of hard bronze."[99

In his rage , he felt justified spiritually and morally, in using his powerful spear and throwing it at the goddess. He struck her beautiful skin, just above her palm. And she began crying and fell her son. Apollo recognized the rage and intervened to shield Aeneas from the wrath of Diomedes. Iris was able to fly over the battleground and saved Aphrodite who was bleeding from the heavenly ichor, which flows through the veins of gods. Diomedes yelled to her while she flew away: "Keep thee away, daughter of Zeus from fighting and war. Is it not enough to say that thou ist the most attractive of weakling women? However, if you are tempted to enter, you'll be shaking your head at the very mention of it, when you hear it from distant. "[10]

While on her journey towards Olympus, Aphrodite came across Ares sitting on his spear in a cloud watching the bloody events below. She pleaded with him to loan her his chariot in order to get to their destination faster and he agreed with her without hesitation. When she reached Olympus she screamed at Achaeans and told all the other goddesses and gods that their sins had no limits given that they were ready to slay even gods. Athena was merely laughing at the gorgeous goddess, then returned to her father and laughed at her. Zeus advised Aphrodite that she was to be in the bedchamber of her marital partner, not in the battlefield, and suggested that her to not take involvement in the battle. The gods of the other gods did not follow the advice. invigorated by the heat of war, they traded illusion for speed in their schemes.

In the meantime, Diomedes's fury did not cease and, when Diomedes observed Aeneas being shielded before him by Apollo and Apollo, he swung his arms at the man three times despite the fact that his efforts were thwarted by the god every time. At the end of the fourth assault, Apollo turned to him. In a loud scream Diomedes was reminded that He was not immortal and had nothing to do with their glory or value. Diomedes's anger dwindled for a moment and he surrendered to gods when Apollo carried Aeneas off to the temple of Apollo on Pergamus. In Pergamus, Leto and Artemis awaited the hero's return and healed him within the sacred sanctuary.

While the battle raged beneath, Apollo flew to the cloud that held the demon of the human race and cursed

Ares in allowing the Diomedes to take such freedoms in the face of gods. Ares still was there, leaning against his spear with the stoicism that only the God of War could display in the midst of an acrimonious battle. Apollo addressed him with the words "Ares, Ares, thou curse of mortals, blood-stained stormer of walls will thou not enter into the fight and then withdraw this man out of the battle the battle, that son of Tydeus who is now willing to be fighting even against his father Zeus? "[11]

Ares was in agreement along with Apollo the idea that Diomedes's actions had gone too far and was in need of control. Apollo took off to meet his sister and mother at his shrine on Pergamus While Ares arrived in the Trojan troops disguised as the head among the Thracian allies. With his voice, that of Acamas He began criticizing those Trojans who were incapable of keeping an Achaean in check. His words of wisdom rekindled in the hearts of others and they turned their attention to their chief prince Hector.

The Achaeans also showed their strength as well, and Diomedes was able to turn to his allies, with Odysseus on his side, and instilled in them a renewed enthusiasm for the war. The battle resumed and was unmatched in terms of brutality. Aeneas returned to his troops when Apollo noticed that Athena was gone from the battlefield. He was not certain exactly where the goddess went however he was sure that Aeneas was secure from her interference and he was aware that the Trojans urgently needed him.

With Ares by with him Hector attacked the Achaeans and killed them in a flurry however, it was Diomedes that saw through the Thracian disguise. He turned to his soldiers and commanded them to surrender ground. Like the foolish Paris or Aeneas, Hector too had the help of a god -- only his god, the God of Warto aid them in gaining an unfair advantages. The Achaeans were adamant about Diomedes' words and surrendered while avoiding their enemies with his hated assistance.

At Olympus, Hera turned to Athena and drew Hera's attention back to Ares's ill-conceived actions, and then rebuking her as god of war. "Out onto it, child of Zeus who bears the aegis, unwearied and to no avail that we made our commitment to Menelaus and that it would not be until he was able to sack the his well-walled Ilios will he bring back home, if we were to endure the wrath of Ares in his anger. Oh, come to us, and let us be thinking of the ferocious courage of. "[12]

Athena saw the queen of gods, and she acknowledged that Ares was going too far and needed be stopped. The goddess went straight to the temple of Zeus and saw her sparkling armor, sporting a fierce Aegis which would inflict terror into anyone who could see it. When she was there she looked towards Zeus and inquired if He was in agreement with Ares's actions, considering that Zeus had declared himself to remain neutral throughout the entire process and refused to decide the most beautiful of goddesses by himself. "Then in response, she addressed her Zeus the cloud-gatherer "Nay, come now and rouse him Athena the who is the driver of the spoil who has been known over others to inflict sore hurt upon him. .'"[13[13.

Athena left Zeus on his throne in awe and bored. Hera was riding her chariot and was waiting for her. They flew towards the field and, after which, in disguise of the Stentor, the warrior Stentor, Hera called out to the Achaeans who were by her flank. "Fie the Argives! basic things of shame, fair to a mere resemblance! For as long as Achilles was known to be a good soldier in battle, never would the Trojans appear in front of the Dardanian gate, because of his great spear been dread. But they are now away from the city, they are fighting against the hollow vessels. "[14]

The Achaeans were driven to such a far distance from their city, they were fighting on their ships, anchored on the shore where they spent the last 10 years. They were attracted by the words of the goddess and began fighting to defend themselves. Athena looked over at Diomedes who was scrubbing the blood from a minor wound he'd sustained from Pandarus and was scolded by Diomedes. Athena informed Diomedes that he'd forgotten the name that his dad Tydeus had and that he probably was no longer a descendant of this great warrior if he were unwilling to leave the battlefield in such a manner. Diomedes saw Hera as being the legendary woman she was and advised her that it was futile to participate in the battle when Ares was fighting. Athena was scolded by him for being scared and informed the man that Ares had promised Her and Hera that he'd come down to the battleground in aid to the Achaeans. It turned out that it turned out that Ares was averse to the

Greeks and was in favor of assisting those his love, Aphrodite, supported.

Diomedes was now standing on his fast chariot and the axels groomed as Athena was seated alongside Diomedes. They pursued Ares and, when the god realised that Diomedes was about to strike his back and was about to strike him, he launched a spear towards the massive soldier. Athena was able to catch the spear with one hand, , and then helped Diomedes take the hit once they had a good distance. Diomedes's spear tore the stomach of Ares The god's scream was louder than both armies merged. A scream of pain echoed with shock from the god's mouth and he walked off the battlefield in a flash, and emerged bleeding on by the sides of Zeus's father. Zeus.

After that, the battle continued , but without the help of gods. Then, just before the darkness was set night fell, Prince Hector as well as Ajax the Great faced the other in combat. A duel ensued , in which neither side gained an advantage over the other. Although they were even, they continued to fight until the lights were too dim to allow anyone to carry weapons against one the other, and both armies disbanded for the night.

The Achaeans unification of their troops and burned any dead bodies they could take back to their ship, while waiting until the dawn. In the meantime the Trojans disputing bitterly with each other. With Paris within their ranks They demanded that he pay his wife back to Menelaus however, the prince of the day would not accept the request. He offered the prize was taken from Sparta after he abducted its queen, and even more but he was not willing to let go of Helen herself. She was given to him by Aphrodite , and it appeared that nothing but blood from his family members could soften his soul when it was given to her.

The following morning, the two armies signed an armistice to rid the battlefield of their dead and bury the dead in a dignified manner. In

Olympus, Zeus had seen enough gods fighting and had now commanded them to stop fighting any more. From now on, he would observe how mortal heroes reacted to the challenge at Troy.

After the battles resumed, the Greeks were not able to hold their own. The Trojans defeated them to the wall they constructed to protect their ships. After the defeats, Agamemnon swallowed his pride and surrendered to Achilles. He brought Briseis to his tent in hopes of encouraging him back to the fight, but Achilles was unmoved.

Even though the results of nighttime clandestine attacks on sleepy Trojans as well as their compatriots by Diomedes and Odysseus The next day brought even more tragedies to the Achaeans in the ferocious fighting. At the time the day was over there was no sign that anyone was safe from injury within the Achaean camp and included Diomedes, Odysseus, and even the legendary commander Agamemnon. Achilles was curious about the impact of his mother's remarks to Zeus and his godfather, pleaded with his friend Patroclus to accompany him to Agamemnon's camp. While there, the entire throng of hurt and suffering Greeks forced him to convince Achilles to assist them and Patroclus was apathetic towards them all.

The next few days, Achilles was still unmoved despite the Trojans moving further than the Greek defenses and fighting with their vessels. Hera was becoming increasingly annoyed with her husband's reluctance she decided to take action to ensure that the Trojans were not victorious in the battle. "Then she thought about of the queenly, ox-eyed Hera was thinking of ways to influence your mind Zeus that bears the aegis. It was to her the most effective: to visit Ida who has adorned her body with beauty in the event that the desire of the man to lay close to her, and hug her in affection, and she could be able to get a warm and calming sleeping on his eyelids, and his shrewd mind."[15[15]

She contacted Aphrodite and requested that Aphrodite, the god of love grant her her love and wish to accompany her husband to bed. Aphrodite saw no reason not to keep her talents from her queen and was willing to accept. The next night, Hera succeeded in her attempts , and Zeus was sunk in such a deep sleep that Poseidon was able to help the struggling Greeks.

As Zeus awakened, he realized that he was a fraud and not only granted his permission to Apollo to assist the Trojans however, he also sent him to the battlefield for himself. With the help of Apollo and assistance, the Trojans broke through the Achaeans' defensive wall , and were able to reach their Greek ships. At this moment, Patroclus could no longer be able to watch the destruction in silence. The king turned his attention to Achilles and requested him to join the battle , and should he not agree accept, at the very least let him to take on his Myrmidons to fight the Trojans who had began to torch their Greek ships. Achilles eventually agreed to be his friend and offered his armor, to make him fear the Trojans.

Achilles's armor's impact at the battlefront was decisive. Patroclus killed a number of the most skilled Trojan warriors. Seeing they were witnessing their most powerful warrior returning to the battlefield The remaining Achaeans resisted the battle with greater vigor. The Trojans were pushed back to their strong walls while Patroclus took the Greeks to the front. "Then could the Achaeans' sons would have taken high-gated Troy with the help of Patroclus who was seated before him he fought with his sword, had Phoebus Apollo made his way to the wall that was well-constructed, thinking thoughts of a curse for him, and instead offered assistance towards the Trojans. Three times did Patroclus walk on an area of the high wall, and three times did Apollo throw him back, striking the defense with the power of his finite hands. When the fourth time, he ran off like a god, with a terrifying scream Apollo spoke to him with the winged voice: "Give me back Zeus-born Patroclus. It's not destiny I'll tell you that through thy spear this city godly Trojans will be destroyed but not by the spear of Achilles who is more in comparison to thee.'"

The battle for Patroclus was fierce, and each great hero was struck by the wrath of every angle. After taking one step back from the gods, Patroclus fell into a duel with Hector and the two were so evenly matched , they both ended up slipping apart and joining the crowd of soldiers surrounding them. Patroclus faced his foes three times and each time he killed the three Trojan warriors. The fourth time the Trojan warrior Apollo was once more in the maul, and ended Patroclus's victory. He hit Patroclus initially in the rear, knocking him to the ground before he landed across the helmet which sent it crashing out of his face. At this moment the courageous Euphorbus struck a spear towards Patroclus and wounded him, however, Patroclus wasn't yet defeated. He began to withdraw to join his companions, but was discovered by Hector and, after one last swat of the sword, Patroclus lay dead in the shadows of the walls he wanted to tear down.

A relief from the past depicts Patroclus's body Patroclus to be lifted from the ground by Menelaus as well as Meriones whilst Odysseus and other people look on.

Nikolai Ge's painting "Achilles Lamenting the Decline of Patroclus"

Achilles was obviously devastated. The body of Patroclus was reburied to Achaeans' camp and the whole army was mourning the loss of an outstanding soldier. Although they burned his body and enjoyed a meal to honor him, Achilles fasted. His mother Thetis who was aware that Achilles was bound to be killed if he killed Hector and tried again to save her son from suffering. She pleaded with the god of gods Hephaestus to create for Achilles the best armor he'd ever created hoping that it would safeguard him.

A photo of Thetis offering Achilles armor made by Hephaestus.

With the armor, Achilles was able to join the fight however, as he observed Achilles cut through the Trojan army with speed, Zeus knew that he was required to bring peace to the conflict. There was no honor in a slaughter therefore he called on goddess Themis and instructed she to gather the entire caste the gods and lead all of them into his palace. After all of them had arrived, Zeus told them he had lifted his previous prohibition against fighting and urged them to choose whatever side they would like to bring honor and glory to the fight. "So spoke Zeus, the son of Cronos and ignited the battle unabated. The gods walked to fight and were divided in their counsel: Hera gat her to the gathering of ships, along with her Pallas Athena and Poseidon Shaker of Earth and also the aid of Hermes which was above any imagining in his mind. And together with them went

Hephaestus exuding with his strength, and halting however, beneath him his slim legs moved with a swiftness; however, to the Trojans were Ares of the helm that flashed along with Phoebus (also known as Apollo), from the locks without horns and Artemis and the archer along with Leto as well. Xanthus and the laughter-loving Aphrodite."[16[16

People who were on Achaeans' side opened the path for Achilles to strike the Trojans while he hunted for the killer of Patroclus. Achilles killed and tossed the bodies of so many members of those Trojans in the River Scamander that the god of the river was able to rise up and fight his battle, but Achilles refused to give ground. As it appeared Achilles could be a victim of the god of the river, Hephaestus attacked the god with a fury so powerful that Hera had to summon immediately, in order to stop it spreading throughout all the rivers in the country.

The war soon turned into gods and men with each one turning his hands on the other mother against brother, sister against son. Ares with his status as god of war, bringing confidence, went to his goddess of knowledge, Athena in bloody arms. The battle was a bitter one between them until Ares took her down and smashed the sharp edge of his spear onto the Aegis in her chest. But this Aegis was able to shield her from the rage of Zeus himself and Athena struck back with a blow that sent the god crashing through the air. "'Fool Athena,' she said. Athena"'Not yet have thou figured out that thou's strength is greater than what I declare me to be, and that your strength is equal to my strength. In this way, thou shalt be able to satisfy the Avengers summoned by your mother and who, in her fury, creates evil against you since you've renounced the Achaeans, and hast offered assistance to the ever-growing Trojans .'"[17[17

The end was near for the Trojan gods. They were punished by Hera and reminded of their position on

Olympus and instructed to put aside their pride and return into the fold. Hera reminds them of the divine law and then they put aside the battlefield for the mortals, with the exception of Apollo. God was concerned about his Trojans however, and as they returned to their walls He disguised himself and was able to lead Achilles out of the doorways and into the open space. When Achilles finally came out to Achilles after which the doors were locked and everyone, except Hector who was too embarrassed to leave, was safe in the gate. This was to be the last error Hector made.

A fable from the past of Hector's last trip to see the wife of his, Andromache as well as his infant son

Astyanax The infant son is shocked by the helmet of his father.

Zeus thinks about the possibility of saving Hector for the third time however, Athena persuades her father the fate of Hector has been determined. After a brief fight, Achilles killed Hector. Prior to his death, Hector appeals to Achilles to take his body to him for proper burial, however Achilles refuses and mocks him by throwing his body across the dirt , and then the men of his army repeatedly attack the body of Hector. This demonstrates how obsessed Achilles is in anger. Priam and Hecuba are watching from within those city wall, wretched over the death of their son.

"Achilles Kills Hector" written from Peter Paul Rubens

Achilles continues to abuse Hector's body But Apollo intervenes to protect Hector's body against further damage or decay. Apollo eventually convinces Zeus the fact that Achilles must return the body back to Hector. Zeus accepts the idea and gets Thetis for convincing Achilles that this is what he has to do in the meantime, at the sending Iris to inform Priam that he has to take the body of his son. The gods give Priam safe entry into the camp, and the king pleads to Achilles. Priam eventually convinces Achilles to release the body using Achilles' connection to his own father.

When the gods took their off from the battlefield, the war continued in the same manner. Allies joined the Trojans with increasing force and included the army of Amazons with a queen named Penthesilea, Achilles slew and became infatuated with when the bloody helmet was taken off. The gods, who were once split because of pride or an interest they reunited after they witnessed the devastation Achilles continued to inflict on the world and avenged the Patroclus's death however his anger was not satisfied. So, during an assault on the city which Achilles defeated the city's defences, Apollo was given permission to direct an arrow from Paris' bow to hit Achilles in the same spot that Thetis was holding the infant at the River Styx. Achilles was killed however, not by mortal hands which left his honor in tact.

Because the Iliad is a complete story of the ending of the Trojan War, many readers who are not familiar with the epics of Homer or haven't read them for the past have the mistake of thinking that the Iliad closes with the Greeks making use of Trojan Horse. Trojan Horse to capture and destroy Troy. Actually, the dramatic last battle Achilles's death and devastation of Troy all take place in the first chapter of the epic poem Odyssey.

In the last days of Troy Achaeans were given three prophecies to determine their fate. "To be precise, the first was in the event that they could have the remains of Pelops were delivered to them; then, the battle of Neoptolemus was fought and, thirdly in the event that the Palladium was thrown down from the heavens, was taken from Troy and remained there, since when it was within the city's walls, it was not able to be taken."[1818

Odysseus once more took the initiative and made sure every object was recovered, even sneaking through Troy in disguise as a begging man to get the Palladium. Even though he was not the commander in chief of the Achaeans Odysseus made sure that they would succeed in Troy through the creation of the famous Trojan Horse, lamented by Aeneas when he fled his city in flames.

"Ourselves did make

A crack in our walls, and then opened to the outside world

the walls of our city. All and everything

The wheels were reinforced for the task. The wheels were smooth-gliding.

lay beneath its feet. They had great ropes hung around its neck

until we reached the walls, the engine of death climbed

pregnant with women-at-arms. Every side

Fair maidens and fair youths made the song for a celebration,

and swung the ropes with a joyous heart and smile.

And up it went, the tower of doom.

And in a proud and threatening way by our Forum and in proud menace through our Forum.

... Cassandra then

in the heaven-instructed heart, our doom predicted;

However, they were doomed to be awestruck. the sons of Ilium.

The nation that is hapless in its last days

scattered free across the streets and to shrines where they can be seen the flowers of the votive flowers."[19[19.

"The Procession of the Trojan Horse in Troy" from Giovanni Domenico Tiepolo

seventh century BCE representation of the Trojan Horse, the oldest known illustration yet to be found.

The Trojans didn't pay attention to their fate Laocoon and the sons of Laocoon who were slain by a powerful serpent from the sea, after they had warned against bringing the unfortunate horse to the city. After having celebrated their victory, and then sat quietly drinking their drinks afterward, their Greek fleet returned from their hidden hideout on the island nearby of Tenedos then stepped through the cracks in the city wall, and slaughtered their foes who were unaware of their presence. The spoils were split between the commanders, and the mighty Troy city Troy was torn completely to the ground.

After the Achaeans had claimed the land they believed was theirs through divine right, and revenge had been imposed from his memory Hector by removing his son Astyanax out of the city walls, they fled. Every leader returned to the kingdom of his own, and generally speaking their fates was theirs to decide. What happened to Agamemnon, Odysseus, and Diomedes during their time in the Trojan War afforded them fame and fame and the gods decided to take the decision to not take revenge for what transpired there.

What happened after the war, anger, rage, and slander at each other and the demarcation between "war" as well as "return" was an indulgence that the gods could not grant Ajax the Lesser. In the course of looting cities, Ajax the Lesser not only declared that the goddess of prophecy Cassandra as part of his bounty, she was also raped at the altar of Athena. This is why Athena made sure he didn't return to his home, slamming his boat onto the rocks, sealing his fate, even fate if merited.

Chapter 13: Logistics

It might be helpful for readers to examine the military tactics of this time period in order to comprehend the larger story. One of the major concerns is the "Ten Years Gap" in between Greeks making their way to the beach in Troy and then burnt it all down. Because very little seems to have occurred during this time and the response to the question of "prophecy" was a step beyond the realms of the fantastical and the fantastical, this issue was that was debated by the early Greeks and others. Following the time that Herodotus composed his Histories which were as full of fantasy like The Iliad, Thucydides wrote the more sane History of the Peloponnesian War. It is famous for not having any mention of prophecies or gods the Thucydides's interest was the political maneuvers and extremely real-life logistics of war. He came to a clear conclusion on the reason Troy's city Troy wasn't captured as quickly before: "And this was due not so much to the scarcity of soldiers as it was due to the lack of money. The difficulty of subsistence saw the invaders cut down the number of their army to a level where it could remain in the country for the duration in the conflict. Even after the victory that they achieved upon arrivalwhich a victory it was likely to have been, or the fortifications for the naval camp couldn't be builtThere is no evidence that their entire force being used. On the contrary they appear to be reverting to cultivating the Chersonese and to piracy as a result of shortage of supplies. This is what allowed the Trojans to hold the field for a decade against their enemies; the dispersal of their enemies made them always an equal opponent to the detachment they left behind. If they had carried plenty of supplies and continued to fight the war , without sputtering out for piracy or agriculture, they could be able to defeat the Trojans in the field as they would have been able to compete with the unit on duty. If they had held on to the siege, the capturing of Troy could have required less time and effort. However, the lack of funds has proven the weaknesses of earlier missions, so it is the same for the one at issue, more well-known than its predecessors, might be judged by the proof of what it did to be inferior in comparison to the opinions it arising from the instruction of the poets."[20[20.]

The method of warfare used throughout the Iliad is often a source for confusion for readers too in part because it is not to be confused with the one used for those who fought the Spartans at Thermopylae as well as the Athenians during Marathon. Hoplite warfare, which was the type of battle that was used during the time of The Greeks throughout the Persian Wars in the Classical period, is illustrated by the phalanx-like formation in which soldiers fought using spears and the shields that were interlocked (known in the Greek language as "hoplons," after which the type of warfare is known as).

The strategy employed during the Trojan War is very different however, and is a perfect fit for to the needs of the story more than any tactical advantage for the military. The warriors of The Trojan War also generally fought in one-on-one combat, particularly when they were the greatest heroes. This is also an art of telling stories; applauding the phalanx's coordination isn't as exciting as the duel battles which occur several times throughout the Iliad. The duels among Paris and Menelaus For instance, the duel between Paris and Menelaus permitted the narrator to praise the combat abilities of each soldier, and also to announce the divine intervention which would prompt each arm to take on the other after 10 years.

In the epic there are several instances of chariot battles (when Diomedes fights Ares For instance) as well as an ongoing theme in the pre-hoplite war. If the option to purchase armor was an expression of pride and standing -- and given the events in the Iliad in which the soldiers battled against the armour of a fallen comrade it is evident that this was the casethat is why the possibility to purchase a chariot have been a semblance of awe for anyone riding in the. This would have been obvious to the reader of ancient times.

Chapter 14: Myth, Legend, or Folktale?

The historical significance of the Trojan War and the account in the Iliad is of course crucial. Are we expected by the modern-day reader to believe that the old readers or listeners believed Apollo struck Patroclus on the back causing him fall and die? Do we need to accept that the ancients too took their stories with a pinch of salt? These are questions that are similar to the bodies of hydras, they are constantly generating more questions as the answers are tried until they finally reach the massiveness such as "What does religion mean?".

In the present, there is little doubt that a combat did take place at an area in Turkey which is most likely Troy. In the many decades that separate the battle from the present there are numerous sources linking Troy to the region, and there's an abundance evidence of "historicizing" of Troy in the Iliad in itself. However, arguing about the exact location or even existence of the battle is taken for granted in the context of the legends that are contained in the Iliad In this epic work, the story of that of the Trojan War is considered to be a true legend.

Folklore scholars of Grimm's fairy tales However, they know how difficult it is in distinguishing some stories as "legends" while others are "folktales." Fantastic stories acquire the qualities of flypaper over their lifetimes They develop in time and space and transform. They undergo slight changes each time a new version is told within the oral culture. For instance, the rise of the "wicked stepmother" in Grimm's collection of fairy tales was a result of the first publication of the tales drew numerous complaints from mothers who were concerned that the majority people who were "evil" protagonists were women, which led to the idea of making them stepmothers instead. [22]

In a quick study of the Iliad and later sources on the war, it's clear how the story could have been altered to serve entertainment purposes, which resulted in its enduring characteristics. The role played by the gods in the narrative that tells the story of Trojan War is most interesting in that it marks the culmination of their creation as entities. Their main function is of "stimuli" to inspire heroic action. The story opens with Zeus seeking to inspire heroic acts, presumably for the sake of his own pleasure. Instead of acknowledging her victory in winning Paris's verdict, Aphrodite ignites the fire of conflict by giving Paris the wife from the person who failed to pay her respects. In the ensuing time, divinities and gods begin flying down to help their favourites and when it comes to Paris's battle with Menelaus and Menelaus, they prolong the war that is already dragging on. The gods are utilized by Zeus to initiate an equilibrium, to eventually to end the war he hoped to end. But ultimately they only add a sense of grandeur to what is basically the story of a legend of an imagined historical moment. [24]

It's also simple to lose track of the time these mythological or mythological people "lived," and not surprising, considering the nature of mythology as well as its role in the historical and cultural aspects of our lives There is a lot of confusion about the exact timeframe. However, reading Hesiod's Ages of Man can help to broaden the perspective. According to the Hesiod poem Works and Days, written in the seventh century BCE (the same time that Homer's writings) Humans have gone throughout the five "stages" of their existence:

It was the Golden Age. The Golden Age was the time when Chronos's reign before Zeus. The people of that time was free of struggle and toil and were able to live to a very old age, passing away peacefully and being in the form of spirit beings (daemons).

It was the Silver Age. The people of this age was not longer than the preceding generation, however their childhoods lasted for more than 100 years. The event occurred in the time of the transition in the reign of Chronos and the son of Chronos Zeus However, mankind was unclean and Zeus defeated them due to the fact that they did not believe in the gods.

It was the Bronze Age. The time of the Bronze Age was when humanity was at its most savage and most aggressive. In the midst of impiety and an inclination to fight against one another, Zeus destroyed this generation by a great flood. There was only Deucalion along with his spouse Pyrrha lived to tell the tale.

It was the Heroic Age. A majority of the heroes that are linked to Greek myth were born in this period following the flood but prior to the "common" human age. The heroes remained in harmony with gods and participated in the epic battles of Thebes as well as Troy.

It was the Iron Age. This was the time period that Hesiod believed that he lived. He puts it down in the context of a time that are free of work, full of fantasy heroic acts of deeds, as well as the ever-present (and frequently visible) presence of gods. It's, in essence, what he calls the "debased" age filled with drama, despair and disappointment.

The tale of the Trojan War is essentially the tale of men fighting against the divine impulse and, therefore, the background of these men within Hesiod's setting should be highlighted. It is worthwhile to highlight the timeline that characterized The Heroic Age in this case because the tales within generally focus on the major "tribal" families that were part of The Mycenaean Palace Period, centering around places like Argos, Mycenae, Thebes, Athens, Aegina, Claydon, Iolcus, Corinth, Sparta and Crete. These centers of culture gave rise to the stories of Greek mythology, beginning with the flood. Deucalion was able to survive until

Agamemnon's battle in Troy. Stories like that of Danaus inspired the tale of Bellerophon and the birth of Perseus to Danae and Zeus later on. Additionally, the tales of the Perseid Dynasty, which started with Pelops who was the son of tragically ill-fated Tantalus and resulted in the tales about Atreus as well as his brothers Agamemnon as well as Menelaus. It is important to keep to mind that tales of Troy weren't the first regarding the devastation of the town by Greeks; Hercules had sacked the city a generation before. This unclear chronology explains the location in and the "historical" time to the battle in the thoughts that of early Greeks and an underlying thematic structure of the gods of the ancient Greek religion.

Actually, in the time of the Trojan War, particularly the incidents depicted in the Iliad The gods are depicted "with the least amount of fantasy possible" according to the historian G.S. Kirk stated. "They can be supermen or superwomen who have special capabilities of instant travel as well as remote operations - they provide an additional dimension of action and a powerful source of inspiration."

Chapter 15: Themes

Kirk conducted research on the Greek myths in light of those of the surrounding cultures. He reached a variety of interesting conclusions that illuminate the role played by gods in the myth that took place during the Trojan War. The ancient roots of their origins go back to the beginning of the cosmos, Kirk stated that the natural development and detachment of gods from their first "nature-gods" constitute the main aspect of the mythical activities of gods. "As gods" the author wrote, "once they have achieved their shape and function, they have a limited scope of actions."[2626

Writing about the similar at the same time, Homer and Hesiod formalized and established the power of gods. There are also elaborations written by playwrights who later wrote in Athens including Euripedes however, at the time of the Trojan War, the roles of myths have been established to such an extent that their actions serve in the form of elements that contribute folklore-related themes.

Kirk breaks down the most commonly used themes from Greek Heroic myths into 24 categories. Five themes he believes to be specifically related to major myths (such such as "Enclosure or confinement in a jar, chest or tomb"). The other five are related to disagreements in the family, like "Deceitful daughters" which don't actually concern the history that is The Trojan War. The remaining are all incorporated in The Trojan War, including the most mythological or folkloric aspects.

Tricks, riddles and clever solutions to problems. Of course, there is a name that springs to mind when the word "ingenuity" is discussed in the same manner as a myth: Odysseus. In his quest to solve Tyndareus's dilemma up to his discovery of his creation of the Trojan Horse, Odysseus is in the same league as Oedipus for his inventiveness. Kirk observes that there is an intrinsic value to this story that is the reason it is featured in numerous Greek myths, and indeed numerous folktales from all over the world.

Transformations. There are some unclear moments when gods are talking to humans, but they typically take the form of an animal (a swan in the case of the birth of Helen) or a warrior, on either side.

The accidental killing of a family member or lover. This theme is best illustrated by the time Achilles finds love with his female companion as the legendary Amazonian soldier Penthesilea.

Giants, monsters, snakes. The brutal finale involving Laocoon's demise is a defining part of the epic tale of Troy's demise. They usually signify the presence of a natural power of the chthonic, but the Greeks were more inclined to taking the form of the monsters (multi-headed or snake-like) from mythologies from their Near East that permeated their society long before the writings of Homer.

Achieving a goal or a fulfilling a requirement or. This theme is at the basis of the Trojan War myth.

Contests. They are called the Judgement of Paris results in Paris winning Helen as well as Aphrodite taking home an Apple of Discord.

Punishment for immorality. This theme is evident in the actions of all three goddesses following the verdict of Paris, which includes Aphrodite's vengeance against Menelaus.

Aiming to kill or killing the child of one's own. This theme is illustrated by the way Agamemnon is attempting to murder his child Iphigenia.

Retribution by killing children of a man. Based on one interpretation of the story the murder of the son of Hector Astyanax can be a good example, instead of being merely the act of taking the possibility of revenge.

Special weapons. Thetis's fear of her son's safety leads to her trying to provide him with the most effective equipment made by Hephaestus. the description of which fills an entire chapter of the Iliad. [27]

Seers and prophets. This summary version about the Trojan War would have been impossible without the numerous instances of prophecy. The seer Calchas is the only one in charge of a lot of the first decisions made by Achaeans.

Mortal lovers of gods and goddesses. Anchises's relationship with Aphrodite doesn't just leads to her fleeing to the battlefield in order to defend her son Aeneas and her son Aeneas, but also is the foundation of one of Rome's mythological foundations.

Unusual births. Helen's place in the narrative of war extends over the notion that she is incredibly gorgeous. Since she was she was the child of Zeus Helen's beauty was beautiful. This widely used narrative tool is used to great effect here due to the beautiful beauty and Aphrodite's gift that she gave to her husband, the Greeks were able to forgive Paris's behavior to a certain extent.

Another element that is folkloric is added to the story of the Iliad that is the repetition. In the story, Diomedes and Patroclus are depicted as "falling upon" their adversaries "three time" as well as being "rebuffed" after the fourth occasion. This repetition is likely an omen of the Iliad's origins in the oral traditions. Similar to many folktales that are told, the Iliad uses the number 3 to stimulate memorization and create tension in the narrative. Patroclus came upon his adversaries and was killed "three time three" Trojans before he was knocked down by the god, contributing to the narrative concept of fighting the soldier who is not successful, just as Achilles was following the demise of Hector.

The tale about"the" Trojan War, unlike some older myths, may be taken not as a means of determining deeper meanings, such as the societal issues (death and the reasons for natural phenomena such as earthquakes and lightning) or the beginning of rituals associated with cults however, it can be used as an exercise in analyzing storytelling themes and techniques. By studying the myth in a method that is thematic, the modern person "achieves the understanding the inner core through the description of the external appearances."[29 The story of the Trojan War is a way to understand

Chapter 16: How Would you imagine that the Ancient Greeks Have Worshiped These Gods?

The question is an appropriate one to ask readers of today, especially one who has grew into a monotheistic world. To this person gods from that time of Greeks are unpredictable, unpredictable and mean. They are also envious, jealous, and, for want of a better term human. There have been a variety of theories that have attempted to resolve this issue over the last two centuries, but one particular theory seems sufficient specific to be insightful, but broad enough to encompass all aspects of the religion of the ancient Greeks. The idea was put forth in the work of Jean-Pierre Vernant, who stated that to those who were ancient Greeks, "the gods are not more powerful or omniscient in the same way as they're eternal."[30 The theory is best understood by describing the three-part socio-cultural and theological cycle, which includes the hierarchy and individual "powers," and society.

In the time of the ancient Greeks, Zeus was the top of the hierarchy of natural order. It is important to remember the way he was able to attain the post. Modern scholars do not consider Zeus' pantheon of gods with "natural elements," despite the fact that they are frequently linked (Zeus is linked to thunder, for example). However, they do recognize that the pantheon of Zeus was born of natural forces and was embodied in the clothes of the earliest celestial beings, like Ouranos as well as Gaia.

Zeus had to fight with the father Chronos and wage a war to obtain the power the ancient Greeks gave Zeus. The position of the god of the god family gods was unassailable especially after he defied the prophecies that afflicted his grandfather and father through his deviousness. Every god he encountered was an essential cog in functioning of the cosmic hierarchy.

Two sources of confusion typically arise out of this simplified understanding. The first concern the significance in the realm of destiny or fate in regards to Zeus's place in the highest position of pyramid. People who study ancient history frequently discover Zeus altering the course of fate to suit his own reasons However, at other instances Zeus is seen to acknowledge it is his responsibility to keep his hands tied in the exactly the same way. Vernant said that this was an incorrect understanding of how Greeks perceived fate or destiny. The ancient Greeks considered these forces to be not fixed and dependent on external influences, like the ire or desires of other forces. Zeus could be able to alter destiny in certain situations however in the case of the rescue of his son Sarpedon during the Trojan War, his desire was thwarted by external forces and he was forced to accept the fate of his son.

This is an example that reveals the second zone of confusion the one of Zeus giving power and decision-making to the gods of other gods who are likely to "beneath" Zeus in the cosmic order. One thing to consider to remember is that his victories that earned him the position of exalted status to which he was elevated in the first place, were fought hard and usually relying on the support of allies. In Sarpedon's case, Sarpedon, Zeus wanted to save his son. However, Hera said that the gods who were not in the same place were not in agreement, since this could result in the gods each helping their daughter or son according to their own whims instead of, as would be expected for even the god of the gods, the king according to the "natural laws of order." Zeus did not alter how his son was treated as Zeus saw the wisdom in having the gods at his side even though he was superior to each of them, and held the throne in heaven. The connection between the power structure of this god and later feudalism also has its advantages.

It could help the modern reader to see the ancient Greek gods less as individuals rather than as components of the language. The gods of the Greek gods were not just natural phenomena, but also social aspects, their interconnectedness and multiplication being the main factor to their understanding.

The early Greeks did not make a distinction between plural and singular when it came to the context of a specific god. Each god was unique in its own way that were often described through the use of epithets. For instance, if an emperor was asked to do so by an exiled city as well as a criminal looking to get a gentle punishment, the person begging was likely to wrap arms around the king's legs , and call out Zeus Soter, or "saviour." The mortal king then took his divine power, and later elevated status in society due to being aware it was Zeus Basileus, "the king," resided within him. When the king took his troops into fight, Zeus Promachos often known in the form of "pro-war," stood by his at his side. The attributes of Zeus are just a few that Zeus was, and each of them being both gods and element of the god.

To understand this, we need to think of gods as gods of the gods that represent the cosmic elements of the universe which are constantly present and in conflict. Vernant provided an illustration of the early Greeks linking Zeus to the heavens and at the same time making a distinction among two different areas of the sky. According to the ancient Greeks the skies were divided in two parts: the "constantly bright" and unquestionably incorruptible Aither and the Aer one, which is "the area of atmospheric phenomena, whose unpredictable violent nature is of primary importance to people, as it is the cause of the wind, clouds and beneficial rain and also destructive storms."[31 Knowing this double-standard with regard to Zeus helps us comprehend why he started the most intense war that we have ever seen simply to see his heroes realize their full potential.

Each god was associated with a distinct type of knowledge and power and the conflict and rivalry between them is the cosmic order according to how the early Greeks observed it. It is certain that the ancient Greeks loved the tales about Zeus and Hera disputing and fighting, but they "saw the universe as a whole, shattered by contradictions, tensions and conflicts over prerogatives and power."[32However, the tense tensions all occurred under Zeus's universal law of unity, guaranteeing that the return of Chaos could never happen.

The role of gods in society was both a demonstration and active. When it came to being assertive, the gods fought to establish the unchangeable and natural but heavenly order that was created among the common people. Zeus was the godhead of the pantheon, as King was the city's head and a father was the leader of a family. There was an orderly hierarchy that had to be enacted to allow to allow the Polis (i.e. city-state) to work. The hierarchies had

Gods (Theoi) on top of the ladder, Theoi at the bottom, the Heroes (and Daimones) below them as well as Daimones and the "Blessed dead" spirits beneath the Heroes and the mortals who lived at the lowest on the ladder. In addition, recollecting the distance between the person reading the tale of Troy (which has only grown since the time of the Classical Philosophers) and the heroes they were reading about, could assist the modern reader to discern between the tale and their private or public spiritual beliefs.

The vital aspect of gods of social religion included their roles in daily life of religious worship. Religion was a way to integrate the various elements of the individual within the larger society. These "powers" such as love justice, war joy, justice in each person and every aspect of society, and a person who was deficient of any of these abilities was thought to be risky. In one instance Aphrodite was punished by Menelaus because of not committing the gifts he promised her. This is both an illustration of the erratic nature in the "Aphrodite Power" and also an ominous warning to anyone disregarding this aspect of their identity. "[The gods epithets] make possible to incorporate human beings into diverse socio-cultural groups each having their own method of functioning and its own structure and integrate these groups of people into one another to the nature order which is then as a element of God's order."[33[33]

The gods' incarnations as powers were seen in all walks of life, but particularly in the realm of politics. In the case of women who were legally barred from participating in the political arena, there were also rituals that brought people away from the polis and to the wild. These events were centered around the more "personal faith," such as the Bacchic rituals as well as those of the Eleusinian Mysteries.

The cosmic structure is composed of esoteric forces that influence and form a structure, which is replicated and manifested on the earth. Ancient Greek theological cycle can be best described by Vernant's remarks: "The Greeks knew perfectly well that the monarch was not a power of nature, and that the nature of a force was not identical to a god. They nevertheless considered them to be interconnected, linked, distinct aspects of one God-like power."

www.ingramcontent.com/pod-product-compliance
Lightning Source LLC
Chambersburg PA
CBHW071839080526
44589CB00012B/1056